For You

Andreas Seidl

Handover of Power

Global Version

Volume 9: Social Market Economy

Imprint

Bibliographic information of the German National Library:
The German National Library lists this publication in the
German National Bibliography; detailed bibliographic data
are available on the Internet at http://dnb.dnb.de.

© 2022 Dipl. Pol. Theodor Andreas Seidl

Cover: Christiane Ebrecht
Translation: DeepL, Cologne
Production and publishing: BoD – Books on Demand,
Norderstedt

ISBN: 978-3-7568-1339-1

Acknowledgements

My thanks go to my family and friends who have made me who I am today. Special thanks to all those who supported me in writing this book. I would like to thank all my classmates, teachers, fellow students, lecturers, demonstrators, activists, colleagues, companies and countries with whom I have had the privilege of sharing the experiences from which all the ideas in this book have emerged. I would like to thank the staff of Books on Demand for their kind helpfulness. I thank the citizens of Seligenstadt for the harmony and solidarity in which I was able to write.

Foreword

This policy concept contains a variety of proposals for possible political reforms. It can be peacefully and democratically adapted to any current political system of any state in the world, but also to political systems in families, clubs, associations or companies. Wherever humans make or submit to rules that manage living together, the following proposals can be helpful. Readers who find the proposals so helpful that they would like to implement them together with like-minded people can contact the author. The contact form on the last page can be used for this purpose.

Faults and defects
I ask for your understanding that this volume was not professionally proofread. I could only afford professional proofreading for the summary. Spelling errors and unfortunate phrasing may therefore occur. As soon as this volume has sold enough to pay for a professional proofreading, it will be done. After that, a new edition will be published.

English version
Please understand that this volume has been translated automatically. I could only afford a professional translation for the summary. Poor wording and spelling errors may therefore occur. In case of doubt, the German version shall prevail. As soon as this volume has sold enough to pay for a professional translation, it will be done. After that, a new edition will be

published. It was more important to me that no one in the world should have an information advantage than individual translation errors in the complete work.

References
If something has been quoted directly, it is set in italics. If the headings contain footnotes, the sources for direct and indirect quotations apply in the chapter for which the heading stands. Otherwise, quotations or source references are directly at the word or at the end of the sentence or paragraph. This book contains parts of text based on the Federal Constitution of the Swiss Confederation of 18 April 1999 (as of 12 February 2017), abbreviated to BV[1] and the Constitution of the Canton of Bern of 6 June 1993 (as of 11 March 2015), abbreviated to KV[2].

If the constitutional paragraph, or individual paragraphs thereof, are based in whole or in part on extracts from the BV or KV, this is indicated in a footnote. The references to the corresponding footnotes for constitutional paragraphs are usually found after the heading of the affected chapter and sometimes in the body of the text. Articles used in the Swiss constitutions are listed in the footnote with a number after the title of the constitutional paragraph. Example: §123 Sample title: BV Art.123, KV Art.123.

All internet sources are fully cited in the footnotes. They were last accessed on 30.09.2021. All literature sources are also listed in full in the footnotes.

All references to tasks undertaken by other ministries and described in more detail there are given in footnotes. Example: Model Ministry - 1.2.3 Model Chapter.

All footnotes are to be viewed in comparison to the respective source, so-called indirect quotations. Direct quotations are set in italics, but hardly ever occur. The source reference is intended to enable further investigation and to take copyright

---

[1] This is not an official publication. Only the publication by the Swiss Federal Chancellery is authoritative. https://www.fedlex.admin.ch/eli/cc/1999/404/de On 14.12.2021
[2] This is not an official publication. The Bernese Official Collection of Laws is authoritative. https://www.belex.sites.be.ch/frontend/versions/2420?locale=de#ART71 On 16.12.2021

into account.

Table of contents

1 Goals of the Ministry for Social Market Economy

The Social Market Economy represents a life of security and prosperity in the four economic forms. The highest goal in the Social Market Economy is the common good. The competition of the Free Market Economy is contrasted with a community of solidary entrepreneurs, employees and customers. These voluntary market participants agree to rights and obligations in order to achieve a higher level of social security for all participants. The aim is for entrepreneurs and employees to feel good about their work and to support each other in their self-fulfilment at work. Entrepreneurs have the freedom to start and run companies without fear of financial ruin. The goal of the Social Market Economy is considered to have been achieved when as many profitable companies as possible are founded and managed, innovation and job satisfaction are high, and prices rise less than wages.

2 Departments

The departments are divided into sub-departments and enumerations are usually considered as their individual units. Many tasks of some departments are completely taken over by other ministries as a service.

2.1 Central Department

Part of the Central Department is the Reception Office with the Courier and Mail Room, which directs all concerns, broadcasts and visitors to the appropriate place in the ministry.

2.1.1 Staff

The Human Resources Department is responsible for staff development and planning. For this purpose, it takes care of the recruitment of junior staff, intern and trainee programmes as well as the selection procedures for employees and special selection procedures for applicants with disabilities. For politicians and employees, the department prepares a job plan.

In all its tasks, it works in voting with the personnel board.[1]
All other personnel matters are transferred to the respective ministries. The Ministry of Education is responsible for the training and further education of employees for the state service.[2] The Ministry of Labour takes over the service law.[3] This includes the labour and collective bargaining law for employees in the state service, remuneration, personnel administration of all careers and employees, flexitime, holiday and sickness records, working time with or without flexitime in part-time or full-time at the place of work or in home work. The Ministry of Infrastructure provides housing assistance for all state employees.[4] The Ministry of Finance's Pay Office takes care of employees' salary, expenses, travel and relocation costs.[5]

The Ministry of Education provides childcare for all employees in the state service.[6]

The Ministry of Health is responsible for the occupational health service.[7] It ensures occupational health management, deals with the treatment, education and prevention of occupational accidents, controls and provides occupational health and safety through the health auditors[8] of the Company Auditing Agency[9] .

2.1.2 Organisation

The ministries of media, security, justice, finance, labour, state organisation provide audit services for quality management in the ministry, evaluation of work performance, revenues and expenditures, as well as corruption prevention, sabotage

---

1 Ministry of State Organisation - 2.1.1.1 Personnel board
2 Ministry of Education - 2.1.1.1 Education and training for the state service
3 Ministry of Labour - 4 State enterprises, 13 Labour Directory
4 Ministry of Infrastructure - 2.1.1.1 Housing assistance for state service employees
5 Ministry of Finance - 2.1.1.1 Staff remuneration
6 Ministry of Education - 2.1.1.2 Childcare for state service employees
7 Ministry of Health - 2.1.1.1 Occupational Health Service
8 Ministry of Labour - 20.7.2 Health auditor
9 Ministry of Labor - 20 Company Auditing Agency

protection and, if necessary, disciplinary matters.[10]

The language service for translating talks or texts is provided by the Ministry of Education.[11] The Ministry of Finance organises the annual budget vote and ensures proper accounting in each ministry.[12] It regulates budget procedures, budget law, staff budgets, departmental budgets, costs and cash management, and assists ministries in budget planning for the budget vote. The Ministry of Labour regulates procurement law and ensures corruption-free state orders and procurement.[13]

The Ministry of Digital Affairs supports the supply of Information Technology.[14] In voting with the Procurement Office of the Ministry of Labour, it takes care of the procurement, provision, maintenance and service of technical devices and software. Much of this is produced in-house to ensure data protection in information and communication technology. Information technology and digitalisation officers audit and advise the ministries. Digital appointment calendar and documentation services are provided as well as a digital policy archive including a library.

2.2 Management Department

The Management Department is the minister's department. With his office team, he provides policy planning and analysis for his ministry and coordinates the relationship between the nation and the municipality through exchanges with his deputies in the municipalities. He initiates cooperation with other ministries or citizens in committees and is supported by the Ministry of State Organisation.

The Ministry of Media Affairs, through its media service, provides press and public relations for the ministry, moderates civil dialogue, trains or provides a spokesperson for the minister, writes speeches and texts on request, and ensures the

---

10 Ministries of Media, Security, Justice, Finance, State Organisation - 2.1.2.1 Audit services
11 Ministry of Education - 2.1.3 Language Service
12 Ministry of Finance - 8 state revenues, 9 state expenditure
13 Ministry of Labour - 6 Procurement Office
14 Ministry of Digital Affairs - 2.1.2.1.1 Supply of Information Technology

implementation of conferences and events.[15]

The Ministry of Digital Affairs is responsible for digital management and thus provides departmental management. It automatically produces business statistics, staff surveys and the current state of research through statistics. It automatically forwards proposals to the affected or empowered state employees. In document management, it ensures digitalisation and that ministries share forms with each other.[16]

2.3 Department for Economy and Enterprises

The Department for Economy and Enterprises ensures the formulation of draft laws and the execution of laws for Social Market Economy companies. This includes, in particular, cooperation with other ministries, insurance companies and collective bargaining partners.

It oversees the execution of the economic order and economic development. Economic development is supervised by economic data from the ministries of Labour, Economy, Finance, Innovation, Digital and Foreign Affairs. With the help of this data, the long-term stable growth strategy is continuously adjusted in cooperation with the Minister of Social Market Economy and the head of the note issuing bank. Agreements are coordinated in cooperation with the Antitrust Agency.

The Department for Economy and Enterprises oversees the execution of cooperative and democratic management and the negotiation of collective labour agreements. It oversees whether the laws on the employment contract, employee protection and insolvency are having the desired effects. If they do not, it works in cooperation with the Minister for Social Market Economy to amend the legislation accordingly. In the event of a disaster, the Department for Economy and Enterprises coordinates the conversion of production of suitable Social Market Economy companies in cooperation with the affected ministries.

---

15 Ministry of Media Affairs - 2.2.1.1 Media Service
16 Ministry of Digital Affairs - 2.1.2.1 Digital Service

2.4 Department for Economic Sectors of the Social Market Economy

The Department for Economic Sectors of the Social Market Economy, in cooperation with the Ministry of Labour, develops the labour law requirements for the state service and the awarding of state orders to Social Market Economy companies. It reports private educational institutions to the Ministry of Education and, in voting with the Antitrust Agency, assists Non-profit companies in forming cartels.

In the real estate sector, it provides for the rights of buyers and sellers of real estate and coordinates tenancy law negotiations between the Tenants' Association and Landlords' Association. It ensures the operation of the caretaker service and the organisation of Residential Community Exchanges.

In the finance economy, it coordinates cooperation with the Ministry of Finance, especially with the Central Bank, the Financial Supervisory Authority and the People's Bank[17] . For agriculture, it operates the Farmer Directory[18] in cooperation with the Ministry of Digital Affairs and ensures exchange with the Food Directory of the Ministry of Labour. In cooperation with the ministries of Planned Economy, Education and Justice, the department provides for crop workers. In foreign trade, the department ensures the formulation of Social Market Economy trade contracts in cooperation with the Ministry of Foreign Affairs. Supervision of foreign locations of Social Market Economy companies is coordinated with the Company Auditing Agency and embassies. Entry permits for guest workers and requirements for imports and exports are coordinated with the embassies and Customs in the Ministry of Security.

2.5 Department for State Services

The Department for State Services coordinates services to companies with the ministries of Labour, Education, Innovation, Digital, Health, Family, Planned Economy and

---

17 Ministry of Finance - 11 People's Bank
18 Ministry of Digital - 12 Directories

Justice. It oversees the operation of health insurance and legal expenses insurance. It ensures the operation of compulsory insurance for parents, the unemployed, pensioners, loss of benefits, economic downturns, insolvency, buildings, buildings liability and household contents.

It ensures the moving in of insurance premiums through business taxes from the Social Market Economy and fees from contributors of other economic forms. It supervises the provision of services and ensures accounting so that tax revenues cover costs.

3 Tasks of the Ministry for Social Market Economy

The mission of the Ministry of Social Market Economy is to create an economic form that is solidarity-based, environmentally friendly and sustainable, and geared towards ensuring social security and prosperity in the domestic market. Solidarity is promoted by running companies on a freelance or community basis. Collaborative management means cooperative and democratic participation of employees in the company, where friendships, children and sports are promoted. Solidarity between employers and employees is demonstrated by the equal establishment of collective labour agreements through democratic negotiations and employment contracts with defined rights and obligations.

In order to promote a sustainable economy, the Ministry of Social Market Economy enacts laws on employee protection so that one can survive a working life unscathed. In the event of insolvency, the ministry operates an insolvency insurance scheme that handles company closures in a socially acceptable manner. It is one of the many compulsory insurances with which the ministry covers illness, parenthood, unemployment, pension, legal protection, loss of benefits and economic downturns.

The Ministry of Social Market Economy fulfils the task of ensuring an environmentally friendly economic form through its stricter laws on environmental protection and peasant agriculture, which also cultivates the state green spaces with permaculture.

To promote prosperity, the Ministry of Social Market

Economy operates various economic sectors. In the real estate sector, buyers and sellers are supported through assessors and renovations, tenants and landlords through democratic tenancy negotiations, insurance and a caretaker service. To promote a solidary and sustainable Residential Community, the Ministry organises Housing Exchanges.

The finance economy has the particular task of increasing prosperity inland. This is done by a national currency with its own Note-issuing Bank ensuring price stability. A domestic stock exchange offers investment opportunities that have a particularly low risk of default and can also deliver constant or growing returns in the future.

Agriculture contributes to social security by providing sufficient food and harvest workers to make the yields of the state green areas available to the people. Farmers' welfare is ensured by shifting the entire food value chain from the Social Market Economy to a farmers' majority-owned cooperative.

Foreign trade is geared towards social security inland and avoids locational competition for the lowest taxes and standards through foreign trade regulations.

Through its tax policy, the Ministry of Social Market Economy ensures that it can fulfil its tasks fully and in the long term. Since the Social Market Economy business tax is a profit tax, it is in the ministry's interest to increase the profits of all companies in its economic form. State services are geared to this. They make it possible for companies to be accompanied in their establishment, to receive advice on maximising profits and to be supported in the digitalisation of administration and sales. In cooperation with the state institutions for education and research, skilled workers can be trained and contract work and research assignments can be carried out.

In the event of disaster or war, the Ministry of Social Market Economy has the task of being able to switch the production of all its companies as quickly as possible, for which plans are drawn up and exercises held.

4 Economic policy[19]

The Ministry of Social Market Economy pursues an economic policy that gives companies as much economic freedom as possible, but takes away as much as necessary to ensure social security on the part of entrepreneurs, employees and consumers.

The Ministry of Social Market Economy operates an economic policy that allows the economic form to exist autonomously. The other economic forms can trade with the Social Market Economy, but have no say in how and with whom work is done. The autonomy of the Social Market Economy can be limited by the Constitution and the Ministry of Labour.

4.1 Economic order of the Social Market Economy[20]

One is a member of the Social Market Economy as soon as one opens a company in the Social Market Economy or works in such a company. All persons can be customers of the Social Market Economy. As an autonomous economic form, the Social Market Economy helps to stabilise the economic situation of the country, even if there are economic downturns in another economic form. For humans who have a greater need for social security, the Social Market Economy offers companies in many sectors in all regions of the country. Employees, providers and customers benefit from the entrepreneurs' election to open their companies in the Social Market Economy because they can rely on visible and audited standards, solvency and service delivery.

Small and medium-sized enterprises that are family-owned are particularly promoted by cooperatives, state enterprises of the Ministry of Social Market Economy and the Company Auditing Agency. This promotion provides for exemptions under antitrust law in order to be able to gain similar market power in competition with large corporations.

---

19 §210,1,2,3,5 Principles of economic order: BV Art. 94, KV Art.50
20 §130.2 Cultural protection areas and economic zones: BV Art.50

4.2 Economic development

The overall economic development of the Social Market Economy is studied by making analyses and projections in real laboratories, i.e. in selected or all companies of the Social Market Economy. The key figures of the statistics include the growth of turnover and profits, the development of the demographics of employees, pensioners and applicants of the companies. With the help of the key figures, the ministry conducts economic and structural policy research in cooperation with the Company Auditing Agency and the Ministry of Digital Affairs, which provide the necessary data. The aim of the research is a long-term stable increase in living standards, common good and productivity.

The Social Market Economy offers its entrepreneurs a lot of security and all companies commit to solidarity with other companies in the Social Market Economy. Competitors are also companies in solidarity. They expand their supply through division of labour and exchange or lend out parts, personnel or machines, or buy together to obtain quantity discounts. Companies are supported in start-up, profit maximisation, research and development by the Company Auditing Agency, the People's Bank and the ministries of Social Market Economy, education and innovation. The central point of contact for Social Market Economy companies is the Company Auditing Agency's economic auditors. Each company is assigned a permanent economic auditor, the other auditors are different for each audit.

4.3 Agreements

To take advantage of economies of scale and avoid excessive prices, companies work with the Company Auditing Agency to collude on quantities and prices. Social Market Economy companies are allowed to share their market to avoid overproduction and waste if the responsible economic auditor of the Company Auditing Agency makes a recommendation to do so. Companies are sought that can use waste generated during production in their production chain. Affected citizens can use a quorum of 10% to force companies and the Company Auditing Agency to hold the agreements on quantities and prices publicly on Government Television[21] with the participation of the Minister for Social Market Economy or his or her municipal deputy.

5 Switching between economic forms

The Ministry of Social Market Economy ensures through its requirements that the change of persons, companies, goods, services and financial products does not endanger the Social Market Economy. Entry and exit fees are applied and market entries are audited by the Antitrust Agency to ensure that they do not jeopardise the Social Market Economy. Goods and services, on the other hand, are usually left to the free competition of the market and certified by seals of quality and safety.

5.1 Entrance of persons and companies

Persons enter the Social Market Economy when they start a company in the Social Market Economy, enter into an employment contract with a company in the Social Market Economy or buy products from companies in the Social Market Economy. Entry fees are the cost of higher quality and safety, which increases prices.

Companies can change to the Social Market Economy if they were founded in another economic form. The Ministry of Finance is responsible for the change of business tax.[22] For the audit of changing companies, the Company Auditing Agency carries out special audits.[23] These audits examine which risks the companies pose that could trigger a compulsory insurance claim. Entry fees depend on the economic performance of the company and the likelihood that compulsory insurance could be claimed and the presumed amount of loss. As a protective measure, insurance coverage may only be possible after a certain number of months of premium payments, higher

21 Ministry of Media - 7 Government Television
22 Ministry of Finance - 5.2.7 Business taxes in the economic forms
23 Ministry of Labour - 10.2.2 Changing companies

premiums may be due or a deposit must be paid for a certain period of time.

The Antitrust Agency additionally examines within the scope of the special assessment whether market entry would jeopardise an authorised cartel. The company may then only enter if the time limit of the approved cartel has expired or the approval has been revoked. In negotiations with the affected companies, the Antitrust Agency can adjust the market division so that the company can enter the Social Market Economy.

5.2 Exit of persons and companies

Persons withdraw from the Social Market Economy when they close their Social Market Economy company, terminate an employment contract with a Social Market Economy company, or no longer purchase products from Social Market Economy companies. Exit fees are not charged. Insurances can be taken into other economic forms via the Citizens' Insurance.

Companies withdraw from the Social Market Economy when they change to another economic form. When a company leaves the Social Market Economy, the following special audit by the Company Auditing Agency also determines the exit fees for the Social Market Economy. The amount of exit fees depends on the amount of state services and compulsory insurance benefits claimed, less business taxes and insurance premiums already paid. Exit fees cannot be negative, i.e. they cannot be paid out. Insurance benefits may continue to be received in other economic forms, provided contributions continue to be paid annually.

5.3 Import and export of goods and services

Persons can buy as many goods and services from other economic forms as they want, as long as they can pay for them. They can also sell their goods and services to persons from other economic forms as long as they can find buyers.

Companies are free to source goods and services from other economic forms for their production as long as the standards of the Social Market Economy are met throughout the production and supply chain.

Companies may sell goods and services in other economic forms without restriction. Financial products, such as shares or bonds, on the other hand, may only be sold through the People's Stock Exchange or Ideas Stock Exchange.[24]

6 Enterprise policy

The Ministry of Social Market Economy ensures an enterprise policy that covers all economic sectors. It regulates the principles of business management in trade law, which also includes crafts and trade. The competition policy protects all companies from negative effects of competition, such as loss of performance or insolvency, with the help of insurance. The economic policy of the Social Market Economy gives companies an advantage over competitors from other economic forms. Through the structural policy, all companies are provided with the necessary infrastructure by the Ministry of Infrastructure. The Ministry of Innovation provides support for constant renewal in order to adapt the companies to changing market structures. Through the regional economic policy, companies are supported by the business consultants of the Company Auditing Agency to adapt to their region and to cooperate with other regions. Through the medium-sized business policy, family businesses can be inherited tax-free. Medium-sized companies are given the opportunity by the Ministry of Social Market Economy to merge in order to take advantage of large corporations in profitable areas. Through the consumer policy, companies gain admission to the Company Auditing Agency's consumer surveys and can increase customer satisfaction. This is ensured by certified standards that companies meet with the help of the Company Auditing Agency.

---

24 Ministry of Finance - 11.8 People's Stock Exchange, 11.9 Ideas Stock Exchange

6.1 Liberal professions and trades

All workers who only need their intellectual skills for their work are practising liberal professions. They are So-called freelancers. These are, for example, physicians, architects or lawyers. All professionals who work in the branches for industry, crafts and services are considered So-called tradespersons.

Freelancers and entrepreneurs are obliged to establish a company for their business activities. If they decide to establish their company in the Social Market Economy, they enjoy all the rights and obligations of the Social Market Economy.

6.2 Cooperatives

The Ministry of Social Market Economy regulates the following conditions in the Cooperative Law. Citizens can form cooperatives. This means that all employees pay an entry fee with which they buy shares in the enterprise. In this way, they become participants in company decisions and co-owners who do not receive a salary but a share in the profits. Depending on how many employees a cooperative has and the amount of work done, high initial investments can exceed the savings of the employees. In this case, People's Bank grants a loan for the start-up, which the employees pay off in a savings plan afterwards from their monthly salary, thus repaying the loan. Special payments of any amount are possible at the end of the year. The interest on the loan is equal to the inflation rate plus 10% of the inflation rate as profits for the Ministry of Finance.

6.3 Corporate philosophy[25]

In the Social Market Economy you will find all professionals who value cooperation more than competition. The entrepreneurs tend to be risk-averse and attach more importance to secure and steady growth than to quick profits. Customers place more value on regional and domestic production and services that guarantee social and technical standards than on the

---

25§186.2 Peaceful separation

cheapest possible production and services from abroad with lower standards.

The Social Market Economy consists of companies that operate in a social alliance. To this end, the Ministry of Social Market Economy imposes certain rights and obligations on companies. Companies grant their employees and customers certain rights and standards that are oriented towards the common good. In return, entrepreneurs receive help from the community, which protects them against risks and increases their efficiency.

6.4 Democratic corporate governance

All companies with employees are run democratically. The entrepreneurs can be the founders, owners or managing directors of the company. Founders and owners cannot be elected directly by the employees because at the beginning there are no employees who could be entitled to vote for them. Deselection is also not possible because the founder cannot be deprived of his idea and the owner cannot be expropriated. Owners can be individuals, partners, families or foundations. Companies run by owners and founders are committed to democratic co-determination by employees and customers. If owners decide to convert their company into a joint-stock company, the managing directors are selected by the shareholders in an election of persons process.

The employees, together with the entrepreneurs, adopt a company constitution. The company operates according to this company constitution. The procedure for creating and amending articles is the same as for the state constitution.[26] Co-determination in the company operates with the same procedures as civic co-determination in the state.[27] The managers of all remits are elected by the owners and the employees. As a group, owners and employees each have 50% of the vote. The decisions of the managers can be negotiated

26 Ministry of State Organisation - 9.11 Constitutional Amendments
27 Ministry of State Organisation - 9.10.11.3 Direct legislation, 9.10.11.4 Direct voting

and voted on with the employees through a veto quorum[28] in a company committee. The decisions of the owners or managing directors can only be negotiated in a company committee at the annual general meeting. Owners have the final decision-making right in this respect. A collective bargaining committee can be convened to object once a quorum of 50 per cent of the employees has been met.

6.5 Democratic management

Senior employees form the management in the company. Each manager is responsible for one remit. The remits consist, for example, of research and development, purchasing and human resources, production or services, advertising and sales. Each company is free to choose the number and responsibilities of the departments by voting among the owners and employees. The election procedures for managers are the same as for ministers.[29] The company committees are company meetings attended by employees and owners of the affected company entitled to vote.[30]

6.5.1 Working conditions for managers

The 40-hour week also applies to Social Market Economy managers. In order to nevertheless be able to carry out all management tasks, all heads of all remits form a management cabinet. They elect 2 leaders who take turns chairing the management meetings.

A manager's wages are a maximum of 3 to 8 times the average wage of the rest of the staff. Managers are responsible for meeting the requirements from the management cabinet. The more employees a company has, the more salary a manager gets. If the workload rises above 40 hours per week, another manager must be hired for that remit. If a management activity is performed on a part-time basis, the daily duty periods must overlap by 2 hours so that coordination can take place between

28 Ministry of State Organisation - 9.5.14 Veto quorum
29 Ministry of State Organisation - 9.9 Elections of persons
30 Ministry of State Organisation - 9.6 Committee

the two part-time employees.

6.5.2 Manager in internship

When you become a manager, you have to prove one week of internship in all areas of the company for which you will be responsible. This internship period is repeated every 5 years. Employees from each department brief their manager and give instructions. You are allowed to question the manager's old instructions and make suggestions for improvement.

6.5.3 Ideas for managers

At the end of the internship, all interns express their ideas that they had in relation to the company during the internship and what they noticed about the work processes. The same applies to in-service training and dual students. This is to circumvent operational blindness among managers and fear of termination or disapproval by colleagues, because interns leave the company again anyway.

6.6 Inclusion of disabled people[31]

The companies of the Social Market Economy are committed to the integration of disabled people. The vacancies in a company must first be filled by disabled applicants, provided that the qualifications of the applicants are equal. The companies have the right to ask the health auditors of the Company Auditing Agency for a rating of whether the applicant with a disability is able to perform the job. The Institute of Occupational Health may be consulted for verification. If the disabled person is hired, subsequent Company Auditing Agency examinations will examine whether and how well the disability is compatible with the job. The data is used to create a file in which disabilities are linked to suitable activities. Based on these examinations, health auditors prepare their ratings for disabled applicants.

---

31 §231,1,3 Integration of disabled persons: BV Art. 112b

6.7 Environmental protection[32]

Social Market Economy companies guarantee high standards of environmental protection. They are certified by the health auditors of the Company Auditing Agency that they operate in an environmentally neutral manner. Exhaust gases, waste water and waste must be treated and disposed of or recycled in an environmentally neutral manner. Environmentally neutral means that all production materials must be biodegradable within 2 years. Prior to biodegradation, processing and recycling steps may be required, which must be known and affordable. The price of processing or recovery must be priced into the product or service. Products must consist of recyclable, replaceable and repairable parts.

Devices must not be built in such a way that they break down more quickly. Even if this results in a production price that is up to 20% higher, the companies' devices must be built in such a way that they function for as long as possible and are as easy to repair as possible. In case of doubt, a minimum service life of 15 years is the requirement. A 10-year guarantee applies to all Social Market Economy products that are not consumer goods.

6.8 Childcare[33]

Parents are allowed to bring their children to work. In every work building, it must be possible to convert a room into a children's room. To equip the room, toy boxes can be ordered from the procurement office[34] or lent out from the municipal libraries. Toy boxes are put together by the Ministry of Education to select age-appropriate educational toys and purchase them inexpensively in collective orders. There are three types of boxes for children aged 0 to 4, 4 to 12 and 12 to 18.

The parents in the work building with the children's room organise themselves in a childcare rota so that there is always one parent from all the parents in the building with

32 §190.8 Environmental protection
33 §234.4 Children's rights, child benefit and parental protection
34 Ministry of Labour - 6 Procurement Office

a maximum of 5 children. The other parents can continue working. Childcare time is considered working time and must be coordinated with colleagues in a way that does not disrupt the work flow. If many children are born in a department, another part-time or full-time employee may have to be hired. Within the opening hours of a nearby state nursery school, a company can require its employees to have their children looked after there free of charge.

The state nursery school may not be more than 5 kilometres from the workplace and must accept children from companies in the Social Market Economy. If the opening hours of the nursery school make it necessary, the children may be brought to and picked up from work by a parent. These transfer times are considered working time.

Small entrepreneurs can join together within a radius of 5 kilometres and request a state nursery school as soon as there are at least 10 children to be cared for from all companies. In rural areas, the radius limit does not apply. A transport service from the nursery school is offered to take the children to or pick them up from a specified address.

6.9 Friendship

Employees should be supported in making friends within their colleagues. To this end, regular times are set aside for colleagues to get to know each other away from the workplace. These include company outings, company parties and company-organised leisure activities, such as a drama group of colleagues who perform plays at company parties. Time spent in company leisure activities is not considered working time, but company outings and company parties are.

In the colleagues it should be possible to work with friends at one's own request and to avoid colleagues for whom one cannot feel sympathy. This is not about an immediate compulsion to transfer for the employer, but as soon as the operational process permits and a retirement or termination leaves a position vacant, the request for transfer must be fulfilled.

6.10 Company sport

All activities are audited by the Company Auditing Agency's health auditors and appropriate physical exercises are arranged for the colleagues to do together on a regular basis during working hours. These can also be stretching and relaxation exercises that train the body on muscles, bones and tendons that are strained or neglected due to work.

Employees and owners may establish a company sports club. This makes it possible for a company sports club to use the state sports facilities during closing times or to lend out sports equipment from there.

7 Employee protection

The Ministry of Social Market Economy issues laws on occupational health and safety in the companies. The Company Auditing Agency's health auditors check compliance with health protection laws. The economic auditors check compliance with occupational safety and health laws.

7.1 Dismissal Protection Act

Terminations are subject to time limits and rules that the affected citizens democratically agree with the Ministry of Social Market Economy. The Employment Protection Act[35] serves as a basis for discussion for the committee. Employment contracts may only be limited in time if there is a material reason for doing so. The notice period is 3 months.

7.2 Continued Remuneration Act

Continued payment of wages on public holidays and in the event of illness is subject to time limits and rules that the affected citizens democratically agree on with the Ministry of Social Market Economy. The basis for the committee's

---

35http://www.gesetze-im-internet.de/kschg/index.html

discussion is the Continuation of Remuneration Act[36] .
Holidays and sick days are paid for employees through their
wages. Sick days are covered by the General Health Insurance[37]
from the 14th sick day for entrepreneurs and employees of the
Social Market Economy.

7.3 Holiday Act

Employees in the Social Market Economy are entitled to 30
days' holiday per year. Holiday days can also be paid out in
addition and continue to work. Holiday not taken does not
expire, but the holiday days not taken must be paid out at the
end of the year. Up to 7 days of leave may be taken into the
new year.
Overtime is treated as holiday. However, if overtime is worked
at night between 10 p.m. and 6 a.m. or on public holidays,
it must be rewarded with 20% higher pay. If compensatory
time or leave is taken instead of payment, the overtime hours
worked at night or on public holidays count as 75 minutes.
Leave remains subject to regularisations democratically agreed
upon by the affected citizens with the Ministry of Social
Market Economy. The Federal Leave Act[38] serves as a basis for
discussion for the committee.

7.4 Works Constitution Act

Every company with more than 2 employees has a works
council. All employees are entitled to vote, but are allowed
to cede and reclaim their vote to representations. All works
councils are networked via the Labour Directory. Each works
council is given a group in the company's profile. The works
councils of all companies unify by sector, municipal, national,
continental and international. They communicate with the
labour unions and set the requirements for the workers' side
in collective bargaining.
The rights and duties of the works councils are democratically

36http://www.gesetze-im-internet.de/entgfg/index.html
37Ministry of Health - 5.12.2 General Health Insurance
38http://www.gesetze-im-internet.de/burlg/

agreed by the affected citizens with the Ministry of Social Market Economy. The Works Constitution Act[39] serves as a basis for discussion for the committee.

7.5 Staff Representation Act

All state employees participate in direct democracy in their ministry to determine how tasks can be fulfilled most effectively. The tasks are derived from the ministers' election programmes and the laws and voting of the citizens. Staff representation is guaranteed by the heterarchical way of working.[40] All affected staff members of a ministry decide democratically, together with the minister, how best to implement the people's requirements. The Federal Staff Representation Act[41] serves as the basis for discussion.

7.6 Working Hours Act

The Working Hours Act regulates maximum working hours and minimum rest periods. Anyone who works at least 6 hours must take a 30-minute break. Anyone who works 10 hours must take a 60-minute break. The maximum working time per day is 14 hours, with 10 hours between two working days.

Insofar as so much overtime is worked in a company that a full-time employee could be hired in the occupational group, a new hire must be made. Overtime may be paid out or used as leave.

Working hours continue to be subject to regularisations democratically agreed upon by the affected citizens with the Ministry of Social Market Economy. The Working Hours Act[42] serves as a basis for discussion for the committee.

---

39 http://www.gesetze-im-internet.de/betrvg/
40 Ministry of Labour - 4.7 Direct democratic labour organisation, Ministry of State Organisation - 8.4.3 Internal heterarchy
41 http://www.gesetze-im-internet.de/bpersvg/
42 http://www.gesetze-im-internet.de/arbzg/

7.7 Occupational Health and Safety Act

The Occupational Health and Safety Act provides employees with rights and obligations. The aim is to identify hazards as early as possible and to initiate protective measures. Workers may not be permanently damaged in the course of their work or may only work in a harmful workplace for a limited period of time. If they suffer damage, they must be compensated. Employees must comply with health and safety measures imposed by their employer. Employers receive their requirements from the Company Auditing Agency's health auditors in the audit report.

Occupational safety and health continues to be subject to regularisations democratically agreed upon by the affected citizens with the Ministry of Social Market Economy. The Occupational Health and Safety Act[43] serves as a basis for discussion for the committee.

7.8 Occupational Safety Act

The Occupational Safety Act requires companies to comply with the examinations, vaccinations and requirements of the Company Auditing Agency's occupational physicians and health auditors. This service is Tax-funded for Planned Economy and Social Market Economy companies. Barter Economy and Free Market Economy entrepreneurs can purchase the service from the Company Auditing Agency.

The health auditors work with the entrepreneur and works council to identify and eliminate sources of danger. The costs incurred by the companies as a result of the requirements can be financed through an interest-free loan from the People's Bank. The purchasing department of the Company Auditing Agency[44] procures goods and services to eliminate the deficiencies from the audit. The costs are low because all companies share this service and do not have to employ their own staff for it. Goods become cheaper for all companies through collective orders via the purchasing department.

43http://www.gesetze-im-internet.de/arbschg/
44Ministry of Labour - 20.7.7.5 Purchasing Department

The rules on the requirements and examinations are democratically agreed by the affected citizens with the ministries for Social Market Economy and Health. The Occupational Safety Act[45] , the Load Handling Ordinance[46] , the Infection Protection Act[47] , the Biological Substances Ordinance[48] , Noise & Vibration Control Ordinance[49] , Basic Data Protection Ordinance[50] and the Workplace Ordinance[51] serve as a basis for discussion for the committee. The committee shall include professionally qualified staff from the Institutes of Occupational and Environmental Medicine .[52]

8 Collective labour agreements[53]

In collective labour agreements, companies regularise relations with their employees. This means that wages and working conditions are contractually fixed for all occupational groups in an industry. The employment contract between employers and employees automatically includes all the contents of the collective labour agreement in force. These collective agreements are declared to be generally binding. The principle applies that equal work is paid equally and equal working conditions apply to equal jobs.

8.1 Bargaining partners

In the Social Market Economy, collective labour agreements are negotiated by the two bargaining partners in a sector. The collective bargaining partners in the Social Market Economy are associations of employers and employees. The negotiation process is direct democracy. The elected leaders of an industry

45http://www.gesetze-im-internet.de/asig/
46http://www.gesetze-im-internet.de/lasthandhabv/index.html
47http://www.gesetze-im-internet.de/ifsg/index.html
48http://www.gesetze-im-internet.de/biostoffv_2013/index.html
49https://www.gesetze-im-internet.de/l_rmPICrationsarbschv/
BJNR026110007.html
50http://eur-lex.europa.eu/legal-content/EN/TXT/HTML/?uri=CELEX
:02016R0679-20160504
51http://www.gesetze-im-internet.de/arbst_ttv_2004/index.html
52Ministry of Health - 4.5.5 Institute of Occupational Health, 4.5.4
Institute of Environmental Health
53§228,1,2,6 Labour: BV Art. 110, KV Art.39

association conduct a collective bargaining partnership with the elected leaders of an industry union.

All owners of companies that employ more than 2 people and come from one sector form an employers' association. Employers can exercise their voting rights in the decisions of the employers' association of their sector.

Every worker who works in a Social Market Economy company is automatically a member of an industry union. Employees can exercise their voting rights in the decisions of their labour union. Employees can cede and reclaim their voting rights to an elected works council chair.

8.2 Labour unions

There is a labour union for each industry, and all workers in that industry are automatically members. Opinions are expressed in the works councils which, as a democratic organisation, report the lives and work of all workers to the labour union to ensure equal rights for equal work in an industry. Labour unions take action whenever employers violate employees' rights. In the absence of rights for employees or obligations for employers, labour unions can vote through their members after an initiative quorum[54] in a committee with the Minister for Social Market Economy and all affected citizens. Affected citizens are entrepreneurs, employees and customers of the industry.

8.2.1 Membership fees for labour unions

Labour unions may only charge membership fees to purchase innovative measures or resources negotiated in the collective labour agreement or to acquire voting shares through industry stock. Membership fees may not exceed 1% of the union member's monthly income. The dues are paid by the companies through their business tax. The members of a labour union decide in a committee whether to charge membership fees for a limited period of time or up to a certain amount of money,

54 Ministry of State Organisation - 9.5.13 Initiative quorum

and how high these fees should be.

8.2.2 Umbrella organisation of the labour unions

The umbrella organisation for trade unions in all sectors is the labour union federation. The umbrella organisation ensures that sectoral unions work together rather than against each other where several sectors have conflicting interests. Alliances are made with labour unions in other countries that are in an international union with the inland to align collective agreements. Alliances are also sought between the same branches in other countries. Each sectoral union concentrates on the countries of the world with which its sector is in competition. Depending on the global position of the industry, the umbrella organisation may rise to supranational or international level and represent the interests of employees in transnational collective bargaining and committees.

8.3 Employers' associations

There is an employers' association for each sector in which all company owners in that sector are automatically members. Opinions are expressed in the sector councils, which as a democratic organisation ensure the long-term and sustainable existence of the companies and for this purpose cooperate with the works councils of the companies.

8.3.1 Membership fees for employers' associations

Employers' associations may only levy affiliation fees to purchase innovative measures or equipment negotiated in the collective labour agreement. The membership fees may not exceed 1% of the monthly profits of the company. The companies additionally pay the contribution through their business tax. This membership fee service is free of charge for companies in the Social Market Economy and Planned Economy, but there is a charge for companies in other economic forms.

8.3.2 Umbrella organisation of employers' associations

The umbrella organisation of employers' associations in all sectors ensures that companies work together rather than against each other where several sectors have conflicting interests. Alliances are formed with employers' associations in other countries that are in an international union with the domestic one in order to align collective agreements. Alliances are also sought between employers' associations in the same sectors in other countries. Each employers' association in a sector concentrates on the countries in the world with which its sector is in competition. Depending on the global position of the industry, the umbrella organisation can rise to a supranational or international level and represent the interests of the employers in collective bargaining and committees.

8.4 Collective bargaining

Employer and employee representations negotiate new collective labour agreements for each sector every two years. The content of the collective labour agreement in force may be included in the voting. If a collective labour quorum of 30% of the affected citizens is met, collective bargaining must take place immediately. A vote can change or abolish the periodic election every 2 years to replace it with the collective labour quorum.

Collective labour agreements must be voted on by a majority of all affected citizens before they are valid. Therefore, all collective bargaining is conducted in public and is divided into several steps. In the first step, ideas and opinions of workers and owners are sought directly through the Company Auditing Agency and the Labour Directory bargaining groups, and indirectly through the works councils and sector councils. In the second step, these ideas and opinions are discussed, rated and voted on digitally and in real life. Those entitled to vote are all employees and owners of all companies in a sector. Digital negotiations take place in the collective bargaining groups in the Labour Directory[55] . Real negotiations take place

---

55 Ministry of Labour - 13 Labour Directory

in mobile studios of Government Television on the company premises. In the third step, the 3 most popular proposals are voted on by all those entitled to vote. If there is no majority for a proposal, the Minister for Social Market Economy has the right to decide. He can convene a committee or decide himself. After that, the negotiated collective labour agreement is valid for 2 years or until the collective labour quorum has been met.

8.4.1 Direct questioning

Suggestions for improvement that the Company Auditing Agency collects in its survey forms are passed on to the bargaining partners if the respondents agree and if the suggestions for improvement can be useful for the industry as a whole. Respondents can indicate which information should be anonymised. Queries by respondents or the Company Auditing Agency are always possible and confidential.

As soon as a new collective labour agreement is in force, a new collective labour group is created in the Labour Directory and the past collective labour group is closed. From then on, all entrepreneurs and employees can contribute new ideas to the next round of collective bargaining and have them commented on, rated and voted on with all other entrepreneurs and employees in their sector. All new ideas put forward by employees and entrepreneurs are thus reported, discussed, voted on by the bargaining partners and incorporated or discarded. Workers or entrepreneurs can submit their ideas in real terms in the works council or sector council, or digitally in the Labour Directory.

8.4.2 Indirect questioning

Employees, through their works councils, can forward improvement proposals to the labour union, which brings them into collective bargaining or as an initiative quorum. Owners, through their branch councils, can pass on suggestions for improvement to the employers' association, which brings them into collective bargaining. In the course of indirect consultation, suggestions for improvement are collected and combined so that the leaders of the works councils, sectoral councils, trade unions and employers' associations can use them to develop proposals. The proposals are discussed, rated and voted on in the next step.

8.4.3 Digital negotiations

The substantive negotiations of working conditions are conducted in the Labour Directory bargaining groups in writing through contributions, comments, surveys and voting. In the bargaining groups, employees, entrepreneurs and leading representations of employers' and workers' organisations come together digitally, without being bound to times and rooms. Digital tools include the comment modulator[56] and the wage-price calculator.

Using the wage-price calculator, workers and owners can change the wages and prices of the company they work for. An algorithm calculates the elasticity of demand through the profits and sales figures. Data is retrieved via the Labour Directory and Tax Directory and calculates the scope for changing wages, working hours or working conditions without having to adjust prices. However, prices can also be adjusted in the Wage-Price Calculator. The adjustment can be a fixed amount or a margin within which prices can move. In this way, it can be determined whether excessive wage demands would only drive up the inflation rate.

After all those entitled to vote have entered their desired values in the wage-price calculator, the median of the values is determined and put to the vote of those entitled to vote. Those who vote no here can indicate values above which they would agree. If more than 30% have voted no, there is a second vote in which the median of all the stated values of all no voters is put to the vote. Those who vote No in the second voting must indicate whether they would have preferred the first voting result. Those who voted Yes in the first voting and do not attend the second voting are automatically counted

56Ministry of Digital Affairs - 14.5 Modulator

as having voted Yes again. If there is again no majority of at least 65%, in a third and final voting the wage or the price is entered by those entitled to vote. If an amount is entered for the salary, the price is automatically displayed next to it. If the price is entered, the wage is automatically displayed next to it. Under the price, it is automatically indicated how the quantity demanded and with it the required working hours would change. The voting result is determined by first taking the average of all wage entries and the average of all price entries. These two averages are added together and divided by two. The result is the digitally negotiated wage. It is entered into the wage-price calculator as a wage indication in order to output a non-binding price recommendation.

If the result of the digital negotiation is vetoed by a 30% quorum, a collective bargaining committee shall be convened.

8.4.4 Real negotiations

The real negotiations are conducted in various TV show formats[57] that the affected citizens choose together. On the panel are the leaders of the affected labour union and employers' associations with their negotiators of the currently affected occupational group. In the audience are employees and entrepreneurs of the affected occupational group. The real negotiations are conducted in a mobile studio[58] on the premises of an affected company. The location is determined jointly by the affected citizens. The Government Television sends suitable moderators for the respective show format. All viewers who are among the affected citizens can participate interactively via their People's Computer.[59]

All other negotiations on collective labour agreements conducted by elected representatives of the unions and employers' associations must be filmed by Government Television and made available on the intranet within 12 hours for the affected bargaining group. The bargaining group can

57 Ministry of Media Affairs - 7.2.3 Shows
58 Ministry of Media - 7.1.1 People's Motor Vehicle
59 Ministry of Media Affairs - 7.2.3.5 Solution Finder (Legislation Committee)

then negotiate the video material digitally.

8.4.5 Collective bargaining committee

Strikes are excluded in the Social Market Economy. If the collective bargaining partners cannot reach an agreement, the Minister for Social Market Economy convenes a collective bargaining committee in which all affected citizens negotiate the collective labour agreement in a direct democratic manner. Each bargaining partner must submit at least one proposal for a collective labour agreement to the committee at the outset. In order to collect the necessary data, all affected employees must disclose their wages and working hours for the past year. Companies must disclose their profits and sales figures for the past year. All employees and owners of affected companies are equally entitled to vote. The minister of the Social Market Economy has a veto right, as do the people, provided the veto quorum has been met.

9 Employment contract

In the employment contract, the company and the employee agree on the working conditions in writing before the employment relationship begins. Certain minimum contents are stipulated. The employment contract must contain a job description that indicates the responsibilities of the employee. Remuneration must be at least equal to the minimum wage of 10 Dollars per hour and is set by the collective bargaining partners in all companies with 2 or more employees. Working hours must not exceed 40 hours per week. Between 2 working days, there must be 10 hours of free time. Each employee is entitled to 30 days paid leave per year. All employment contracts are open-ended, unless a material reason can be invoked, which is verified by the Company Auditing Agency's economic auditors.[60] Terminations must be made within the notice period of 1% of the number of days worked in the company. Terminations are subject to the Protection Against Dismissal Act. During the trial period, both parties to the

---

60 Ministry of Labour - 20.7.3 Economic auditor

employment contract may give 2 weeks' notice of termination. The trial period may not exceed 3 months.

Further details are democratically agreed upon by the affected citizens with the Ministry of Social Market Economy. The committee discusses the law on proof of service[61] .

9.1 Obligations for employees

Employees shall perform their contractual work for their employer punctually and diligently. They shall follow their employer's work instructions and make suggestions for improvement. Company secrets shall at all times be kept secret from unauthorised persons. The employee shall not compete with the employer and shall not enter into business competition with the employer in the same market.

Breaches of duty are warned in writing by the employer if consequences are to follow. Repeated warnings are grounds for dismissal. Breaches of duty resulting in damage to property or personal injury may be followed by claims for damages. In cases of gross negligence, the employee is liable. If the employee violates any of these regulations, the employee may be terminated after a warning.

9.2 Duties for employers

Employers undertake to pay their employees in accordance with the agreed remuneration on time at the beginning of a new working week for the previous working week. Employment shall be in accordance with the agreed working conditions and hours. Employees receive the same pay for the same activities and times. This is ensured by the collective bargaining partners through an appropriate classification of occupational groups. Employers have a duty of care and participation towards workers in occupational health and safety. They are assisted in complying by auditors and, where appropriate, by the advice of the Company Auditing Agency and the Ministry of Social Market Economy's insurers. When employment is terminated,

---

61 http://www.gesetze-im-internet.de/nachwg/

the employer must provide the employee with a testimonial. If employers violate any of these requirements, the employee may be terminated without notice.

9.3 Wage

Wages are the same for young and old. The same money is paid for the same work. Age and seniority do not play a role. Work experience can decide on bonus payments or on preferential hiring, but not on wages. Wage developments correspond to developments in the real Gross Domestic Product. Wages are raised or lowered to the same extent that Gross Domestic Product rises or falls.

9.3.1 Minimum wage

The amount of the minimum wage is determined by the Minister for Social Market Economy. The employees of the Social Market Economy can themselves directly democratically determine the amount of the minimum wage by a quorum of 50% and thus change the following sentence in this Minimum Wage Act. The minimum wage shall be 10 Dollars per hour.

9.4 Internship and training contracts

Employment contracts for internships and vocational training are negotiated between the collective bargaining partners and the Ministry of Education. The Ministry of Education takes over the benefits for compulsory insurance. The ministries of Social Market Economy and Education determine further regularisations together with the affected citizens and are guided by the Vocational Training Act[62] .

62http://www.gesetze-im-internet.de/bbig_2005/

9.5 Part-time work

Part-time positions can be advertised and employees can change full-time positions to part-time positions if there are no operational reasons to the contrary. A change notice is required for the conversion.

Further details are democratically agreed upon by the affected citizens with the Ministry of Social Market Economy. The Part-Time and Fixed-Term Employment Act serves as a basis for discussion for the committee.[63]

9.6 Termination of employment

Fixed-term employment contracts end with the expiry of the term. Permanent employment contracts must be terminated in writing or by termination agreement. Both contracting parties can usually terminate within the period of notice and, in urgent cases, without notice.

Employees can terminate their employment at any time and only have to observe the notice period. They can terminate without notice for reasons such as lack of occupational safety and health, serious insults and sexual harassment if the employer had done nothing about it.

Employers can terminate an employee's employment if he or she is performing deficient, has been ill for a long time, is antisocial, disturbs the peace in the workplace, is unpunctual or does not show up for work at all and has already been warned at least twice for such offences. Terminations for operational reasons can be made in the event of a prolonged loss of orders or in the event of a plant closure. In the case of termination for operational reasons, all the companies in the Social Market Economy are in an alliance. They lend out employees and place jobs in other companies of the Social Market Economy in the vicinity. For prolonged downturns, the Ministry of Social Market Economy operates downturn insurance.

Employers can terminate without notice if the employer has committed theft, fraud, unauthorised use of the internet,

---

63http://www.gesetze-im-internet.de/tzbfg/

calling in sick without sickness or working while unfit for work.

10 Insolvency

There is no such thing as insolvency in the Social Market Economy. All creditors, providers, employees and customers can rely on the fact that all services rendered will be paid for and all services paid for will be provided. This is what outage insurance and insolvency insurance are for. Outage insurance ensures that paid services are provided by other companies in the Social Market Economy. Insolvency insurance ensures that services rendered are also paid for.

10.1 Minimum reserve account

Companies must build up a reserve of at least 10% of their company value. They can build up a reserve of 100%. No taxes have to be paid on reserves. As soon as a new company makes profits, the minimum reserve can be built up. This is done by paying part of the profits into the minimum reserve account before tax is deducted. In addition to their tax account, entrepreneurs also keep a minimum reserve account with the People's Bank. Deposits to the minimum reserve account are made automatically before tax is withheld. The owner himself determines the share of the profits to be paid into the minimum reserve account, but at least 10%. Interest is paid on the minimum reserve account at the inflation rate of the national currency.

The minimum reserve slows down growth but increases stability and confidence in the company. If the company grows, the minimum reserve grows; if the company shrinks, the corresponding amount may be withdrawn from the minimum reserve account. Ageing machines and buildings lose value. However, the purchase price is deposited in the minimum reserve. If machines or buildings have to be replaced or renovated, the purchase price plus interest may be withdrawn from the minimum reserve account. After acquisition, the value of the new or renovated machines or buildings must be gradually paid back into the minimum reserve account.

10.2 Insolvency insurance[64]

Insolvency insurance is a compulsory insurance of the Social Market Economy. It is responsible for winding up if a Social Market Economy company is in danger of becoming insolvent and its minimum reserve has been exhausted. A payment is made when a company reports itself insolvent to the Ministry of Social Market Economy. This can be either a report of partial insolvency or closure. Insolvency insurance makes all outstanding payments.

The contribution to insolvency insurance increases in times of good economic activity and decreases in times of bad economic activity. The contribution is 3% of the business tax, 4% in good economic times and 2% in bad economic times. Good business cycle of the company means that the growth of the profits of a company is at least 2% above the growth of the Gross Domestic Product of the Social Market Economy and above the inflation rate of the national currency. Good business cycle of the Social Market Economy means that the Gross Domestic Product of the Social Market Economy is at least 2% above the inflation rate of the national currency. The data comes from the audits of the Company Auditing Agency. Consequently, business tax increases when the economy is good and decreases when the economy is bad. The amount of the contribution is set by the Social Market Economy minister in a committee with the participation of the Company Auditing Agency. The contributions are paid into an account of the Ministry of Social Market Economy at the People's Bank and bear interest at the rate of inflation.

64§150.4 Business taxes

10.2.1 Management consultancy

No later than three days after the insolvency notification, business consultants from the Company Auditing Agency appear at the company and collect all the necessary data. This process takes a maximum of 3 days. After that, a company committee[65] is convened. There, all options are disclosed that are available to the owners and employees in the next 4 weeks. This business advice is about how the company could still be saved in its current form, or how it could downsize to become profitable again, or how a closure should proceed. The Company Auditing Agency's business advisors have access to all the economic data on the intranet and can use the Algoracle[66] to determine the future prospects in the market in which the insolvent company is selling. If the situation is hopeless for the company, the business consultants on the company committee can recommend closure. In the case of partial insolvency, the company committee may vote by majority against closure, but must then bear any costs incurred. In the case of insolvency, this voting does not take place. In this case, the owners must sell the company. The company committee decides whether the company should be sold in parts or in its entirety and to whom.

10.2.2 Partial insolvency

An insolvency does not immediately mean a closure of the company. Each company has 2 individual defaults on payment free, the damage of which does not exceed 500 000 Dollars. Individual defaults are defaults on payments either to creditors, customers, providers or employees.

10.2.3 Closure

As soon as payments cannot be made to at least two parties, the company must close down and be sold in whole or in parts. Creditors, customers, providers and employees

---

65 Ministry of Labour - 20.7.7.3 Company committee
66 Ministry of Digital Affairs - 15.3 Algoracle

continue to receive all their orders and salaries for one month. The insolvency insurance takes over these payments. The employees complete paid orders or, if there is not enough time, they prepare to hand over the business to another company in the Social Market Economy. The outage insurance company takes care of this procedure. The closure of the company is announced as soon as the insolvency has been filed with the Ministry of Social Market Economy. This gives all those affected one month to look for new work partners.

The owners or shareholders receive the proceeds from the sale of the company as soon as all insurance payments have been made and creditors, customers, providers and employees have been compensated. If the sales proceeds are not sufficient to pay all compensation, the insolvency insurance takes over the rest. If this happens frequently, the insolvency insurance premiums increase.

10.2.4 Insurance fraud

Insurance fraud means using either outage insurance or insolvency insurance intentionally to enrich oneself or others. Insurance fraud can also mean that entrepreneurs, creditors, customers, providers and employees do not comply with the requirements of the Company Auditing Agency, which audits, pays out or commissions benefits on behalf of the insurance companies.

Before any insurance benefits are paid out, the Company Auditing Agency checks whether the owners of the company have previously owned a company that had to close or became partially insolvent. Anyone who has used insurance benefits for insolvency or failure several times with other companies will have to pay additional contributions. Anyone who deliberately manipulates to escape the additional contributions also commits insurance fraud.[67]

---

67 Ministry of Justice - 8.5.3 Insurances

10.2.5 Creditor

Creditors are buyers of bonds who have been promised repayment and a fixed interest rate after a fixed term. If a company cannot make this payment, the insolvency insurance compensates the creditors. The compensation consists of the immediate repayment of the full bond amount. The interest payment is suspended from the date of repayment.

10.2.6 Customers

Customers are purchasers of goods or services from the company. Customers who have not yet received a service will be refunded the purchase price. Customers who have already received an incomplete service will be refunded the purchase price less the cost of the incomplete service. Claims for returns or repairs are extinguished for customers after a closure. Customers can claim on the outage insurance and order the same service or the completion of the incomplete service from the Company Auditing Agency.

10.2.7 Suppliers

Suppliers are sellers of goods or services to the company. Suppliers who have not yet performed receive cancellations on all orders. Suppliers who have already performed will be paid the amount specified for that performance. Suppliers who have performed an incomplete service will be paid the amount that covers their costs incurred up to that point. Should the customer not be the closed company directly, but a third party, the outage insurance takes effect.

10.2.8 Employees

Employees are sellers of their labour to the company. Employees receive their wages until the end of the following month. Announced wage increases do not take place. Employees who have compensatory time and holidays must take these days off, as no payment is made. Unemployment insurance applies to employees.

11 Economic sectors of the Social Market Economy

The economic sectors of the Social Market Economy include companies that are privately owned, regularisations for state enterprises based on the laws of the Social Market Economy, and Non-profit enterprises, some of which may organise themselves into cartels.

11.1 State service

State enterprises are managed by the Ministry of Labour.[68] State employees are subject to the same working conditions as all other employees of the Social Market Economy. Customers of a state service have the opportunity to rate the service and make suggestions for improvement at the place where the service is provided or via their People's Computer. If a state service job cannot be assigned to an existing occupational group and sector, it is assigned to the "state service" sector. The employers' association is the Minister of Labour, and the employees' association is the state service branch union.

11.1.1 State orders

State enterprises carry out public orders that are prescribed by citizens or the law. Only if they are unable to do so, a tendering process takes place, after which all companies that have participated are investigated by the Procurement Review Board. The Procurement Review Board is represented by the tax auditors of the Company Auditing Agency.[69]

---

68 Ministry of Labour - 4 State enterprises
69 Ministry of Labour - 20.7.1.3 Procurement Review Board

11.2 Non-profit companies

Non-profit companies are Social Market Economy companies that only want to cover their costs. They mostly serve to promote science, research, education, parenting, art, culture as well as sports and disaster relief. They do not make a profit or they invest all profits in the company. They reduce prices or they pay out the surpluses to the employees. Non-profit companies pay business tax as sales tax at the Social Market Economy tax rate. They enjoy all the rights and benefits of the economic policy in the Social Market Economy and comply with all the rules and standards for companies in the Social Market Economy. Whether a company is Non-profit is checked by the Company Auditing Agency's economic auditors during their regular audits.[70]

11.2.1 Cartels

Cartels are only permitted in the Social Market Economy for Non-profit companies if the supply is inadequate and individual Non-profit companies are in danger of becoming insolvent. In that case, the companies vote with the Company Auditing Agency's business consultants on which form of cartel[71] will support the supply of affected citizens. The legality auditors must examine these relaxations of antitrust law and approve or reject them in voting with the Antitrust Agency.[72] These include the division of customers, sales territories or market shares, as well as price fixing. Negotiations on which cartel may be formed are voted on in a committee of the Ministry for Social Market Economy with direct democratic participation of the affected citizens.

---

70 Ministry of Labour - 20.7.3.5.1 Non-profit audit
71 https://de.wikipedia.org/wiki/Wirtschaftskartell#Kartelltypen
72 Ministry of Labour - 20.7.6 Legality auditor, 20.7.6.9 Antitrust compliance, 15 Antitrust Agency

11.2.2 Private educational institutions[73]

Private educational institutions can offer their own classes as suppliers to the Social Market Economy. Their curricula are not prescribed, only the final papers come from the Ministry of Education and are corrected by its teachers. Otherwise, private educational institutions are not subject to any additional requirements. They do not receive any tax money for financing, but set training contributions. Since the final papers come from the ministry, the degrees are equivalent to the state degrees and are recognised.

12 Real estate sector[74]

The real estate sector in the Social Market Economy is determined by rights and obligations for tenants, landlords, buyers and sellers. The ministry enacts a solidarity-based home ownership and tenancy law. The Real Estate Market in the Social Market Economy is operated through the Real Estate Directory[75] . A profile is created for each property to be rented or sold as a Social Market Economy company. A database is kept in the profile of how high the respective prices have been for all sales or lettings of this property. The rental contracts are stored anonymously in the profile. Interested parties can digitally send rental and purchase enquiries to landlords or sellers via the profile.

The sale and rental of buildings is taxable. Accordingly, every building is considered a company operated by its owner. Social Market Economy business tax is levied on the rental and sale of a property.

12.1 Buyer and seller

The market for buying and selling buildings and land is determined by direct agreements between buyers and sellers. Buyers and sellers of land may only be nationals. To help with price negotiations, the customary local prices per square metre

---

73§178.1 Training contributions: BV Art.66
74§227,1,3 Rental business: BV Art. 109
75Ministry of Infrastructure - 4.5 Real Estate Directory

can be obtained from the Real Estate Directory.

Before each sale of a Social Market Economy property, a Company Auditing Agency technical auditor inspects the property and publishes the inspection report in the Real Estate Directory. Sellers are allowed to defer publication of the inspection report if they wish to take structural measures to improve the inspection result. After the measure has been taken, the property is newly inspected and both inspection reports are published. Each additional inspection is subject to a fee.

Sellers can advertise and sell their property free of charge via the Real Estate Directory. Every sale of a property is taxed at the corporate tax rate. This includes the right for the buyer to have the property extended or renovated and to receive 3% of the sale proceeds for this purpose. This reduces the taxes to 27%. The construction work must be carried out by companies of the Social Market Economy. If the costs for the renovation or extension exceed 3% of the sale proceeds, the remaining amount must be raised by the buyer.

Buyers of Social Market Economy properties have full coverage for the property in any regional disaster. All work to restore the property to its pre-disaster condition is covered. Fixtures and fittings are not replaced. Owners of Social Market Economy property can purchase building insurance and building liability insurance through a monthly premium. Landlords pay for both insurances through the taxed rent.

12.2 Rent negotiations

Because tenants and landlords have a longer relationship, tenants and landlords each form an association. Every tenant is automatically a member of the Social Market Economy Tenants' Association. Every landlord is automatically a member of the Landlords' Association of the Social Market Economy. Tenants and landlords can turn to their association for legal advice and have voting rights when the tenants' association and the landlords' association negotiate rules.

The rules that the Tenants' Association negotiates with the

Landlords' Association in the Government Television publicly and interactively with the viewers apply. The Minister of Infrastructure takes part in this. He can change the rules or prevent them. A quorum of 40% of the population can force the Minister of Infrastructure to determine the rules in a People's Committee.

12.2.1 Rental agreements[76]

In the Social Market Economy, landlords and tenants must abide by rules negotiated by the Tenants' and Landlords' Association. The rules are set out in the standardised tenancy agreement and are available on the Tenants' and Landlords' Association profile in the Real Estate Directory. This tenancy agreement can be supplemented with further paragraphs by landlords and tenants. Landlords may terminate the tenancy agreement at any time in the event of their own need. A notice period of 6 months applies. Tenants may terminate the tenancy agreement at any time with a notice period of 3 months.

12.2.2 Rent control[77]

The rent index is based on the local rent index, which is prepared by the Ministry of Social Market Economy in cooperation with the economic auditors of the Social Market Economy. The rent index is calculated by taking the median of all rents within a radius of 20 kilometres. The rental prices differ depending on how many rooms and how many square metres a property has. Rents may not be more than 10% above the rent index. The rent may only be increased by the inflation rate plus 1% per year.

---

76 §227.2 Rental business: BV Art. 109
77 §227.1 Rental business: BV Art. 109

12.3 Renting

Landlords contribute to insurance and caretaker services through their business tax. Every rental payment is taxed. All rented properties of the Social Market Economy have building insurance and building liability insurance. All tenants have contents insurance. All insurance policies have no territorial limits, so damage is covered no matter where the property is located. The Ministry of Infrastructure does not issue building permits in vulnerable areas.[78]

12.3.1 Building insurance

The building insurance covers the repair of damage to the building caused by storm, hail, flood, fire, lightning or mains water. The technical auditors check the amount of damage and, together with the landlord, determine how the repairs will be carried out. The original condition does not have to be restored, but the costs must not exceed the amount of damage.

12.3.2 Building liability insurance

The building liability insurance bears the builder's risk for construction measures. Construction measures may only be carried out by Social Market Economy companies, as they have outage insurance. Property damage to the building due to gradual exposure to temperature, gases, vapours, moisture or precipitation is remedied by a renovation free of charge. This one renovation may be claimed every 25 years. The renovation costs shall not exceed the value of 1% of the total income of all rents in the building over 25 years. Costs above this are borne by the landlord, costs below this are retained by the insurance company. Property damage from domestic private sewage will be remedied immediately upon application and inspection by Company Auditing Agency technical auditors. Renovation work will be mutually agreed between the landlord and Company Auditing Agency at the time of the inspection.

---

78 Ministry of Infrastructure - 5.4 Building permits

12.3.3 Household contents insurance

Tenants have household insurance that compensates for damage in the event of water, theft or fire. All furnishings are replaced at the original price. If this is not known, a fixed amount is paid for each room. The fixed amount is determined by an algorithm that matches the income of affected citizens in similar areas with persons with similar consumption patterns.

12.3.4 Caretaker service

The caretaker service is a care of the building. The service includes a sweeping and clearing service as well as waste and sewage disposal. If tenants report problems, minor repairs are taken care of. The caretaker service concludes treaties with local service companies or automates the processes as far as possible on its own. The caretaker service is a state-owned enterprise of the Ministry of Social Market Economy.

If companies need security for their premises, it is requested from the local police station. For companies in the Social Market Economy, property protection is free of charge. The property protection is carried out by People's Protection Service staff.

Tenants and landlords can use the Real Estate Directory's brokerage service. The entire pre-selection process is done digitally. Staff from the estate agency service contact tenants and landlords, arrange viewings, pick up house keys, accompany viewings, take delivery of flats on moving out and, if necessary, instruct the Company Auditing Agency's technical auditors to check for defects.

12.4 Residential Community exchange

Residential Communities are several unmated persons, couples or families living together in a flat, house or group of houses. Once a month, the Residential Community exchange is held in each town hall. All seekers come to the town hall and go into a large room. There, the moderator presents photos and videos of the flats or houses and the interested parties play get-to-know-you games together with the landlords or flatmates of the Residential Communities.

The estate agent from the caretaker service shows a presentation via beamer with photos and videos of vacant flats and houses with a view from the inside, outside and on the map as well as the price to rent or buy.

After the presentation of all Residential Communities, all interested parties should get to know each other. For this purpose, new groups are formed every 5 minutes. In a group, a given characteristic is talked about and each participant in the group introduces himself/herself. The first groups are the age groups 20 to 39, 40 to 59, 60 to 80. The second groups represent the status of unmated person, couple or family with children. The third groups are the status in working life, as a trainee, shift worker, self-employed, employee, unemployed or pensioner. The fourth groups are about skills such as DIY, cooking, baking, gardening. The fifth groups tell about the hobbies, such as sports, making music, listening to music, cinema, game nights, computers.

After the round of getting to know each other in groups, all the rooms are presented again in a picture for 2 minutes. During the 2 minutes, all interested parties should go to a corner. There, all interested parties cast their vote on whether this place of residence is their first, second or third election. All interested persons can present their arguments in the group why they would prefer this place of residence. Everyone can be interested in as many Residential Communities as they like.

After all Residential Communities have been briefly presented, stations are set up in the room, one station for each Residential Community. At a station, new Residential Communities can be formed to buy or rent, but also new flatmates for an existing Residential Community can be sought or exchanged.

At the end of the event, negotiations are conducted between tenants and landlords or buyers and sellers. For this purpose, the landlords and sellers come to the respective station. Landlords or sellers do not have to participate in the get-to-know-you games if they will not be living together with the tenants or buyers in the flat, house or group of houses.

13 Finance economy

The Ministry of Social Market Economy regulates the money, credit and financial markets in its economic form. These market transactions are conducted in a national currency of the Social Market Economy. This currency measures the value of the Social Market Economy and makes it possible to distinguish it from other markets and economic forms. The regularisations in the Social Market Economy are based on ethical principles and compliance with all standards of the Social Market Economy. Loans for consumption purposes are prohibited, as are investments in morally questionable companies. The Ministry of Social Market Economy organises committees to formulate the corresponding moral values into laws with the affected citizens.

13.1 National currency of the Social Market Economy[79]

The Social Market Economy trades in national currency, which it issues. The finances of the Social Market Economy are transacted in the national currency of the Social Market Economy. The Ministry of Social Market Economy, the People's Bank and the Company Auditing Agency provide the Note-issuing Bank[80] with all the necessary digital data to determine the current value of the national currency and to calculate the exchange rate. The primary objective of the Note-issuing Bank of the Social Market Economy is price stability. In continental monetary matters, the Note-issuing Bank exchanges information with the Ministry of Social Market Economy and the Continental Central Bank.

All companies in the Social Market Economy accept the national and international currency of the country so that customers can pay in both currencies. Wages are paid in national currency. Goods and services can be paid for in national currency or international currency from the Free Market Economy. Revenues in international currency from the Free Market Economy must be exchanged and paid into the company account in national currency.

---

79 §219.3c Central Bank and Currency Policy
80 Ministry of Finance - 10.4 Note-issuing Banks

13.2 Banking regulations[81]

Social Market Economy banks are subject to ethical financial regulations. Money may not be invested in weapons, food or environmentally harmful forms of production.

The deposits of bank customers are secured by the minimum reserve ratio for banks of 30%. This means that each bank guarantees to be able to pay out 30% of the deposits in the event of a bankruptcy and to secure all accounts with at least up to 100,000 Dollars. This amount is managed through the minimum reserve ratio for banks. The minimum reserve of a bank must always be so high that accounts up to 100,000 Dollars can be paid out in full in the event of a bank failure, and all amounts above 100,000 Dollars at 30%.

Banks receive money from their customers so that customers can save it and banks can invest it. Banks are only allowed to invest the money in companies of the Social Market Economy and in commodities located inland, and only in the two cash currencies that are allowed as means of payment inland. Bonds and shares of domestic Social Market Economy companies may only be sold to domestic bank customers.

13.3 People's Stock Exchange[82]

The Ministry of Finance is responsible for the People's Stock Exchange, which is operated by the People's Bank and creates a national financial market for the state and companies of the Planned Economy and Social Market Economy.[83] This national financial market ensures that the increased money stays in the country so that this money is also spent in the country and increases the wealth of all the humans living in the country. The Ministry of Labour is responsible for the Exchange Commission.[84]

Social Market Economy companies may only issue their shares and bonds on the People's Stock Exchange. Dividends on shares may only be issued after business tax has been paid.

---

81 §217,1,2 Banks and insurance companies: BV Art. 98
82 §217.2 Banks and insurance companies: BV Art. 98
83 Ministry of Finance - 11.8 People's Stock Exchange
84 Ministry of Labour - 18.3.3 Exchange Commission

Only nationals can buy bonds and shares of Social Market Economy companies on the People's Stock Exchange if they have a savings account with People's Bank.[85] Shares must be held on the People's Stock Exchange for at least 12 months. Foreigners may only invest in the domestic funds[86] through domestic Social Market Economy banks and never buy bonds or shares directly.

13.3.1 Investments and returns

The companies invest the money from bonds and shares in the company to generate growth in sales or profits. Companies pay interest on bonds and dividends on shares. The percentage of interest corresponds to the company growth through the bond. The amount of dividends equals the percentage of additional profits generated by the company growth and must not exceed the percentage of wage increase. For example, if the amount of money in the dividend is increased by 10%, the wages of all employees in that year must not increase by less than 10%.

13.4 Joint-stock companies[87]

Companies can be converted into joint-stock companies by their owners. The Ministry of Labour issues the general rules.[88] Social Market Economy joint-stock companies are subject to the special rules of the Ministry of Social Market Economy. Joint-stock companies are characterised by having many owners, So-called shareholders. Shareholders in Social Market Economy companies may only be domestic citizens living in the national territory.

Every shareholder has a right to participate in the management of the company and to share in the profits through dividends. Insofar as losses are posted, the dividend is waived until the losses have been offset by 110%. The employees and owners

---

85 Ministry of Finance - 11.5.4 Savings account
86 Ministry of Finance - 11.11.3 Domestic funds
87 §216.4 Joint-stock companies: BV Art. 95
88 Ministry of Labour - 18.2 Joint-stock companies

jointly decide on the amount of the dividend per share in a direct democratic manner at the end of the financial year. The amount of dividends may not exceed 40% of profits.

The amount of interest on a bond issued by the company is determined by the additional growth in turnover generated by the bond. The amount of interest may not exceed 2 times the turnover growth of the past 2 years.

13.4.1 Shares for employees

Each employee receives a share package corresponding to the equivalent value of his or her job. However, all share packages of all employees together must represent at least 50% of the issued shares. The shares do not belong to the employees, but belong to a workplace in the company. Everyone who works there has the voting rights and benefits from the dividend payments. The voting rights can be exercised at general meetings[89] or lent out to works council representatives. These dividend payments are paid to the employees in addition to their wages and are not taxable.

13.4.2 Shares for machines[90]

Machines that replace human jobs receive the share packages of the job. Machines that do not replace another human's job in a human workplace do not receive a share package. They merely supplement that workplace and increase the worker's responsibility to handle the machine in the best possible way. Dividend payments on shares for machines first pay the machine fees.[91] The remaining dividends go into a fund and are distributed at the end of the year in equal parts per head to all employees of the company as a bonus. Returns from the fund can be invested independently by the company.

---

89 Ministry of Labour - 18.2.1 General meeting
90 §154.5 Tax reduction
91 Ministry of Finance - 6.1 Machine Fees

13.4.3 Shares for savers

Shares that are not tied to employees' jobs can be sold on the People's Stock Exchange. The total sum of the prices of all shares must thereby at least correspond to the residual value of the company. The residual value results from the total value of the company minus the value that the shares of the jobs make up. The issue price of an individual share can be set by the owner.

Each share is a registered share. The name of the owner of a share must be reported to the joint-stock company. Owners of shares in the companies of the Social Market Economy must be nationals.

13.4.4 Stock exchange trading

The initial public offering is handled by People's Bank. It offers its savings customers the shares for purchase from the initial public offering, taking the price set by the owners as the issue price. From now on, the joint-stock company is listed in the index of the respective industry. The 10 joint-stock companies in a sector with the highest enterprise value are included in the Social Market Economy Index.

14 Agriculture[92]

Farmers in the Social Market Economy are committed to caring for the landscape and preserving natural livelihoods. They cultivate the urban green spaces, forests, fields and water bodies with the help of permaculture.[93] The paths necessary for the removal of the harvest should also be open to the citizens for use by bicycle or on foot.

Farmers are the entrepreneurs in agriculture who produce food through land, water and mutual aid. In the Social Market Economy, they price the goods for the end consumer and reduce their costs through a cooperative.

92§220,1b,2 Agriculture: BV Art. 104
93Ministry of Labour - 19.8.7 Nature-based agriculture: permaculture

14.1 Sustainable agriculture

Sustainable means that groundwater and the climate are not polluted, biodiversity is preserved and not displaced by fertilisers, genetically modified crops or pesticides. Therefore, either indoor agribusiness or outdoor permaculture is prescribed.[94] Cultivation should be organic and ecologically sustainable. Organic means, first, growing plants and animals that are as resistant as possible to pests or germs. Secondly, it means building an ecosystem that shields pests or opposes them with beneficial organisms. Ecological means polluting the environment only to the extent that nature can recover from it and reach the initial state before the pollution. Modern aids such as sewage treatment plants and irrigation systems help to keep the pollution and the natural regeneration time low.
The principle of not felling more trees than can grow back applies to forestry. Timber may only be felled at full moon or in winter. This makes the wood more stable and it has to be replaced less often.

14.2 Agricultural trade union

Workers in Social Market Economy agriculture automatically belong to a labour union that asserts the right to fair prices in foreign trade. The same applies to imported foodstuffs that do not thrive inland. Foreign producers, i.e. farmers and their workers, are also union members of the agricultural union as soon as their goods are processed or sold in the country's Social Market Economy.

14.3 Agriculture cooperative[95]

The agricultural cooperative is an organisation of the Ministry of Social Market Economy. All farmers are organised in the cooperative. The cooperative offers favourable services for

---

94 Ministry of Labour - 19.8.7 Near-natural agriculture: permaculture, 19.8.8 Agriculture away from nature: Indoor agribusiness
95 §220,1d, Agriculture: KV Art.51

logistics, operation and processing. All farmers can negotiate favourable prices here in collective orders. If there are no cheaper and better service providers on the market, the cooperative offers logistics, operation and processing on its own.

Operation means the joint acquisition of inputs, such as seeds, fertiliser, fodder or agricultural machinery. The joint purchases are stored in a fleet of vehicles and silos. The farms house these stores. There is only one central warehouse if enough farmers join together and commission the cooperative to build it.

Logistics means the transport from the farm to the end customer. Only reusable containers from the logistics providers are used for packaging. If goods from the farm have to be further processed before they can be consumed by the end consumer, this transport is also taken care of.

Processing means the automated and craft preparation of cereal products, canned fruit and vegetables, fish, meat and dairy products. As producers, the farmers decide who should process their plants and animals as gently as possible. If 20% of the farmers agree, the cooperative sets up companies to process the farmers' food. The farmers remain the owners of these processing enterprises, which are administered by the cooperative on their behalf.

14.4 Harvest workers[96]

Farmers can request harvest workers from the Ministry of Social Market Economy. Through the Labour Directory, all persons who have time are automatically registered and receive a message with an offer. Persons who are always available as harvest helpers are prisoners, Social Villagers and students. Harvest helpers are pupils from the nutrition subject, Social Villagers from the work area luxury supply[97] or prisoners from mobile prisons. The wages correspond to the minimum wage. The farmer pays the wages to the Ministry of Social Market Economy. Social Villagers' wages are transferred to their People's Bank account after deduction of 20% tax for

---

96§220.2 Agriculture: BV Art. 104
97Ministry of Planned Economy - 10 Work area luxury supply

the Social Market Economy and 20% tax for the Planned Economy. Wages for prisoners flow to the Ministry of Justice. Students' wages go 40% to the Ministry of Education, 40% to the child benefit and 20% to the students' People's Bank accounts.

14.5 Farmer Directory

The Farmer Directory is the sales platform for all farmers in the Social Market Economy. Here, end consumers can subscribe to food from a farmer near them. Food of the respective season is delivered all year round. Each farmer is given a profile. On this profile, customers can sign up for a subscription. If the farm is not big enough, the nearest farm is displayed. The farmer can also advertise an extension loan on his profile. Customers can put themselves on the waiting list until they can be supplied by the farmer. Each customer on the waiting list specifies how large the amount of food per week should be. The farmer specifies the cost of an extension in monetary value and food. The customers on the waiting list then have to pay the specified amount monthly or once and receive the corresponding amount of food after the expansion. Farmers can form a group in the Farmer Directory to compile a complete food supply from the region, organise themselves into cooperatives and share seeds or devices.
The Farmer Directory contains all the functions of the Food Directory and its offers are automatically available there as well.[98]

15 Foreign trade[99]

Social Market Economy companies can offer their goods and services all over the world as long as they comply with foreign trade law. The Ministry of Social Market Economy determines imports, exports, foreign locations and the use of guest work in foreign trade law. In the Continental Union's single market, companies are free to choose their locations and labour force

---

98 Ministry of Labour - 19.13 Food Directory
99 §225,1,7 Foreign trade policy: BV Art. 101

as long as the standards of the Social Market Economy are adhered to everywhere. International economic and monetary issues are jointly voted on with the ministries of foreign affairs and labour and the people.

15.1 Trade agreements

Foreign trade of Social Market Economy companies with foreigners is managed by the Ministry of Social Market Economy through tariffs. Trade agreements of many Social Market Economy companies over a long period of time with the same country are negotiated to a committee. Responsible staff from the ministries of Social Market Economy and foreigners, as well as affected entrepreneurs from the countries involved, are entitled to vote in the committee. The resulting template for a trade agreement is put to a vote of the affected citizens. The trade agreement enters into force with a majority of at least 60%.

15.2 Import

Only goods and services that are not in short supply in the country of manufacture and are not produced inland may be imported.

15.3 Export

Goods and services may only be exported at prices that do not prevent the establishment of domestic production in the importing country. Prices for goods and services may not be set lower by domestic citizens in the exporting country than in the importing country.

15.4 Foreign locations

Production may only take place in countries that are in an international union with the inland. All standards that apply in domestic locations also apply abroad. The Company

Auditing Agency also audits foreign locations.

15.5 Guest work

Companies are allowed to hire guest workers if no domestic applicant can be found for the job, even though the salary is above the pay scale for this occupational group. If nationals have to live in Social Villages because they cannot find work in the Social Market Economy, these nationals should be asked if they want to retrain for the required occupational qualification. The period until nationals have the professional qualification may be bridged with guest workers. The guest work contract must be limited in time accordingly. The other rules for guest work of the Ministry of Free Market Economy apply.[100]

Guest workers may not be used if there is a shortage of workers with the guest workers' qualifications in their country of origin. The Ministry of Social Market Economy receives reports to this effect from the embassies of the Ministry of Foreign Affairs. The Social Market Economy is ethically oriented not to cause damage to other countries, but to grow together.

16 Tax policy[101]

The Ministry of Social Market Economy sets business taxes at 30% of the annual profit of each company in the Social Market Economy. However, this percentage is flexible. The less the compulsory insurance is used, the lower the percentage and vice versa. With downturn insurance, premiums are adjusted to the business cycle. The percentage must be high enough so that all state services provided by the ministry can be financed with it or through fees. Companies that have opted for the Social Market Economy receive most state services Tax-funded. The tax includes the flat rates for compulsory insurance and special services provided by the ministry for Social Market Economy. These include costs for occupational

100 Ministry of Free Market Economy - 12.2 Guest work
101 §150,1,3c,4 business taxes, §154,3,5 tax reduction

health and safety measures as well as certification of standards for fair trade, ecological production and high quality by the auditors of the Company Auditing Agency.

Due to increasing automation, business taxes are more and more becoming a fee for operating machines. This fee pays for the Unconditional Basic Income. Citizens who receive it can decide to claim the Social Market Economy's insurance benefits. This reduces the Unconditional Basic Income by the contribution rate.

The operation of People's Innovation Companies[102] is used to be able to reduce taxes as part of the annual budget vote. When People's Innovation Companies are sold, they are converted into companies of the Social Market Economy and pay business taxes until they are sold into the Free Market Economy or closed.

16.1 Profit tax

Business tax is due as profit tax. The Company Auditing Agency digitally audits the companies for profits and losses on a monthly basis. The tax auditors work with the economic auditors to do this. The business consultants work with the innovation auditors and the companies to increase profits. This service is included in the taxes.

17 State services

State services in the Social Market Economy are extensive and mostly Tax-funded. The Ministries of Labour, Education, Health, Finance and Digital Affairs support the Ministry of Social Market Economy in providing state services. The other ministries are remunerated by the Ministry of Social Market Economy. Accordingly, the Ministry of Social Market Economy collects the business taxes or fees to finance the services. The Ministry of Social Market Economy accompanies the companies from start-up to closure.

Economic policy issues concerning the labour market and social order are regulated in voting with the ministries of

---

102 Ministry of Innovation - 10 People's Innovation Company

labour and economy. The fundamental issues of the welfare state and a social world of work are regulated by the Ministry of Social Market Economy together with the Ministries of Labour and Planned Economy.

17.1 Setting up a business

Anyone wishing to set up a company in the Social Market Economy should report to the town hall of their place of residence at the office of the Ministry for Social Market Economy. This is where the initial advice is given on what measures are available and what rights and obligations come with a company in the Social Market Economy. The measures consist of a loan from the People's Bank, a market and operational analysis by the economic auditors of the Company Auditing Agency[103] , an intranet site and website with information and sales functions, and a complete solution of insurance, digital management programmes and bank accounts with the People's Bank.

Each new company is assigned a Company Auditing Agency business consultant for the first 12 months of existence, who audits the business figures monthly and contacts the entrepreneur in case of negative developments. The entrepreneur can contact the advisor at any time with questions. If there is a lack of sympathy between the advisor and the entrepreneur, both can ask for transfer or replacement up to 3 times. In case of any complaints against the Company Auditing Agency, entrepreneurs report to the Town Hall at the office of the Ministry of Social Market Economy.[104]

17.2 Profit maximisation

The Company Auditing Agency audits Social Market Economy companies every 2 years announced and every 2 years unannounced, ensuring an annual audit. The audit consists of a visit to the company premises with a view to

---

103 Ministry of Labour - 20.7.3 Economic auditor
104 Ministry of Labour - 20.7.7.6.2 Business start-up support

compliance with labour rights, health protection and useful work input by all employees. The workers are asked in a questionnaire about their satisfaction at work and whether there are any suggestions for improvement. Company figures such as turnover, profits, costs for machines, materials, labour, advertising, distribution, prices, production and sales figures are digitally audited. For this purpose, the entire staff of a company is recorded in an organigram.

An algorithm calculates the workload for the company, the most successful utilisation of all workplaces, the currently most favourable purchasing opportunities and the behaviour of consumers and competitors since the last audit. An operational and market analysis is created from the data of the company and its market participants. As soon as the audit report is ready, deficiencies and suggestions for improvement are discussed with the staff by an economic auditor in a company committee. In the discussion, the elimination of the deficiencies and the implementation of the suggestions for improvement are determined.

The Company Auditing Agency audits all companies for compliance with the rules and advises them if there are ways to increase profits without having to raise prices.[105] The audit report contains concrete proposals for solutions on how efficiency could be increased. The proposals come from the auditors of the Company Auditing Agency, from the Innovation Database or from the success model programme. The economic auditor makes an offer to management to accept the proposals and discusses implementation and financing.

If management decides against a proposal by the Company Auditing Agency to maximise profits, the Company Auditing Agency can convene a company committee and have all employees vote on it.

---

105 Ministry of Labour - 20.7.7.6.4 Maximising profits

17.2.1 Success model programme

The economic auditors of Company Auditing Agency[106] look for profitable and innovative work processes or production methods during their audit. The entrepreneurs or employees can also point out successful workflows to the auditors during the audit. Successful work processes are included in the Success Model Directory[107] by the economic auditors. Companies can also refuse to be included in the Success Model Directory and instead make an entry in the Innovation Database. If other companies can also use a success model to make their work processes more profitable and innovative, the economic auditors will propose the appropriate success model.

The company that has developed the success model sets a price for it and receives it as a one-time payment from the companies that also want to implement the success model. Insofar as several companies already have successful workflows or have developed them together, they jointly determine a price for it. The economic auditors have a right to propose a non-binding price recommendation. The minister of the Social Market Economy has a veto right with which he can change the prices. Success models become free of charge for companies of the Social Market Economy after 10 years and may also be sold into the Social Market Economy from then on.

Companies that offer and have purchased success models are examined by the economic auditors in a success study to see whether the models are also successful. Companies that introduce and implement a success model are certified on an ongoing basis. The success study and certification of other companies does not take place if the success model has been included in the Innovation Database. The Minister of the Social Market Economy can force companies to share their success models with other companies in the Social Market Economy. In return, the business taxes of companies that have to import a success model are increased by 1%. This additional business tax revenue is transferred to the company that invented the success model.

---

106 Ministry of Labour - 20.7.3.5.11 Marketing success models
107 Ministry of Labour - 20.9 Success Model Directory

17.3 Educational institutions and companies[108]

The Ministry of Social Market Economy, together with the Ministry of Education, ensures that companies can benefit from state education.[109] The companies can have simple work, seasonal overtime and peak workloads taken care of by the educational institutions. This measure is intended to avoid fixed-term employment contracts or terminations for operational reasons. Research projects can mean incalculable expenses for companies. The partial or complete implementation of research projects by the companies with the educational institutions should keep the costs for research and development calculable.

For educational institutions, the high proportion of practice in the educational programmes ensures better understanding and more accurate career prospects for graduates. For companies, this saves on labour costs and for educational institutions, it saves on the hypothetical construction of cases on which to practise what has been learned.

17.3.1 Curricula[110]

Companies are asked by the Ministry of Social Market Economy which contents in the curriculum are relevant to their needs. Representations of employers' and workers' organisations from the respective sectors are involved in negotiating the curricula. Different sectors are involved depending on the subject taught or the educational qualification.

17.3.2 Further education[111]

If companies lack skilled workers, employees or applicants can be trained to become skilled workers through the qualification of volunteers in further training courses. Companies in the

---

108 §180,6,7 Schools and colleges: KV Art.44
109 Ministry of Education - 4.9.2 Cooperation between educational institutions and companies
110 §177.2 School system
111 §182.1 Further education: BV Art. 64a

Social Market Economy can register employees of any age for further training in all state educational institutions. The companies themselves decide what content is to be taught. In continuing education, no entire educational programmes are taught, but rather excerpts from any number of subject areas. Learners can attend individual lessons, take part in performance records or simply learn and practise the content through digital education in the Knowledge Directory and only take the final test at the educational institution.

17.3.3 Work orders[112]

The ministries of Social Market Economy and education draft joint training regulations and set working conditions in collective labour agreements with the unions and employers' associations.
Companies can report to the Ministry of Social Market Economy work assignments that they would like to have done by the educational institutions. Companies can propose in which subject the work order should be done, or the ministries of Social Market Economy and Education can determine specific subjects for industries. The teachers of the subject coordinate with the company and decide in a meeting of the teaching staff of an educational institution with the company management in which year group and subject the work order can best be done. School subjects and study subjects have practical parts in which production or a service is provided for or with companies of the Social Market Economy. Entrepreneurs send employees to the classes of the educational institutions to present the company and the work assignment. The educational institutions fulfil the work assignments as part of the lessons or as part of an examination performance. The work assignments can also be fulfilled by the pupils and students on the company premises. As a general rule, the companies are responsible for machines and materials and must provide and pay for these things. The work performance of pupils or students is remunerated with half of the minimum wage. The dispatch of the completed work

112§177,2 School system, §181,3 Vocational training

order is organised and paid for by the companies.

Vocational schools and colleges receive old production lines from companies. Orders can be completed on them and new creations of the learners' own can be developed in projects and final theses. These end products are presented to the companies from which the discarded devices originate.

17.3.4 Internships

Internships are offered in all schools and colleges during the holidays. The vacancies for internships of Social Market Economy companies are published in the educational institutions and presented at a fair in the educational institution. At the beginning of a new school subject, training course or degree programme, 2-week internships in companies must be carried out during the holidays of the first learning year. These internships are unpaid and are intended to give an overview of the occupational field, building on the knowledge of the school subject.

17.3.5 Vocational training

Social Market Economy companies can offer in-service training at vocational training colleges and colleges for young professionals. Depending on the field of specialisation and qualification requirements, more or fewer hours per week may be worked in the company or at the educational institution. Remuneration may be 20% below the wage of the collective labour agreement. Companies can choose schools and colleges with which they would like to work. Pupils and students can choose companies and activities they would like to get to know.

17.3.6 Research assignments[113]

Social Market Economy companies have the right to commission research from schools and colleges. These can either be orders for basic research or research projects that concern a product, a production method, service or workflow. Similarly, only parts of a company's research project can be carried out with state educational institutions. The research projects can be carried out either in the company or in the educational institution by teachers and learners. The research funds are financed by the companies, and the basic necessities for the laboratories are available in the educational institutions. Further special machines can be lent out or purchased by the company.

The ministries of Social Market Economy, Innovation and Education coordinate which company awards which research contracts to which educational institution.[114] Companies can indicate one or more educational institutions of their election when submitting the research assignment to the Ministry of Social Market Economy. Teachers and learners can select from the research assignments those that best fit into the curriculum or most closely match interests. Research assignments can be carried out at individual educational institutions on a short or long-term basis.

Large or urgent research projects can be carried out over a short period of time in all state educational institutions with a suitable subject area. The ministries of Social Market Economy, Innovation and Education decide in a committee which research projects are to be carried out throughout the country in order to be able to determine the significance for the entire population. Only research projects with nationwide relevance are carried out by all educational institutions in the relevant subject area. Suitable Social Market Economy companies are included in the state research projects and may be required to cooperate.

113§180,6,7 Schools and colleges: KV Art.44
114Ministry of Innovation - 5.2 Research institutions, Ministry of Education - 11.7.4 Research projects with companies

17.3.6.1 Performance records and theses

The colleges conduct research free of charge for companies in Social Market Economy and Planned Economy as part of the students' training. Companies provide proposals, colleges offer courses on the topic and have solutions prepared by all students as a performance record to complete the course. At the end of the semester, the companies receive the best performance records and final papers.

The names and addresses of the originators are listed on the theses so that the companies can connect with the student for enquiries or recruitment requests.

17.3.7 Career fair

Career fairs are annual events at state educational institutions that are either tailored to one subject area and one occupational field or cover all occupational fields that can be learned at an educational institution.

At the career fair, companies present their job vacancies and research assignments, as well as vacancies for interns, young professionals and graduates. The companies can be local or come from all over the country. In any case, every company for which orders are fulfilled in the educational institution comes to the fair, as well as every company within a radius of 20 kilometres that has vacancies. The target group is pupils and students who are currently studying at the educational institution or have graduated from there.

The career fair takes place at the educational institution, where owners and employees of companies can meet possible future applicants. Getting to know each other is arranged in three different ways. First, there are stands where companies present themselves with their jobs, work and research assignments. Secondly, there are short interviews in rotation and thirdly, there are tasks in the classrooms that fit the occupational field. Companies and applicants can exchange business cards with each other. Anyone who hands out a business card expresses their interest.

17.4 Intranet and computing power

On fundamental issues of competition policy in digitalisation, the Ministry of Social Market Economy ensures that companies can use the intranet, computing power and programmes of the Ministry of Digital Affairs. This gives Social Market Economy companies a competitive advantage. The Ministry of Digital Affairs offers all services free of charge to Social Market Economy companies. The costs are covered by the revenues from the business tax and paid by the Ministry of Social Market Economy to the Ministry of Digital Affairs.

Data that is only sent and received within the company at the same location is not stored centrally. However, companies can use central storage free of charge. Companies can use the intranet to digitalise their administration. The possibilities range from production to sales.

Employees can use their identity card as a company badge when entering the company premises, giving them access and entry rights on the company premises that are adapted to the respective workplace.

Personnel files can be viewed via the workers' profiles in the Labour Directory. By indicating on the worker's profile that he or she works for a particular company, the worker authorises that company to access the worker's personnel records for a limited period of time. The access rights end when the employee is terminated or dismissed.

Treaties concluded by the company via the intranet are always automatically notarised and negotiable in court.

Machines can be connected to the intranet in order to be able to transport data securely through the country. Each machine can be created in the company's profile in the Labour Directory. The serial number and operating programmes are read and fed into the Labour Directory algorithm for the most effective use of all devices.

17.4.1 Digitised administration

Digitised machines and employees can manage companies digitally and simulate future company decisions. Similar to a strategy game on a PC, the numbers for employees, machines or prices can be changed to calculate the most successful winning strategy.[115] The algorithm of the Algoracle accesses the entire data of the company and the intranet in order to be able to design the company management like in a video game. Owners and employees have game rights. The company's interiors can be digitised via the indoor virtualiser[116] . Machines and workers recorded in the Labour Directory are recognised by the camera and assigned to the location as the place of work. The activity is determined via the work contract and digitally reproduced. If the activity cannot be retrieved via the Knowledge Directory database, it can be recorded by the indoor virtualiser.

17.4.2 Digitalised distribution

Sales can take place via the company's profile in the Labour Directory. Similar to a digital shopping shop, customers can order goods and services. Delivery services for goods must be Social Market Economy companies. Payment is made automatically via the customer's VAT account and the company tax account at People's Bank.

This digital shopping shop on the intranet can also be downloaded as an internet version so that it can also be operated on the internet. If the same assortment is also to be sold on other current internet sales portals, the assortment can be saved and converted to the format of the internet sales portal. To update the data, a synchronisation can be requested from the Ministry of Digital Affairs free of charge. Centrally at the Ministry of Digital Affairs, the data is transferred from the intranet to the internet with a short delay. All the necessary data is transferred from the servers to a converter, which decodes the data for the Internet and then uploads it

115 Ministry of Digital Affairs - 15.3 Algoracle
116 Ministry of Digital Affairs - 14.7 Indoor virtualiser

to the Internet. The same procedure in reverse order applies to the intranet.

17.5 Compulsory insurances[117]

The Ministry of Social Market Economy regulates insurance law for its companies and insurance companies. It operates the insurance companies necessary for compulsory insurance. Social Market Economy companies pay insurance premiums for their employees and owners through their business tax. This includes insurance against accidents, illness, unemployment, litigation, loss of benefits, old age and economic downturns. Through an increase in business tax, a company can also pay into the insurance policies for parenthood and occupational disability. Each worker and owner decides on this himself and indicates this decision via his profile in the Labour Directory. Wages or profits then decrease accordingly because the tax burden increases by a fixed amount.

Those who do not work in the Social Market Economy can also take out the insurance policies. The contribution period is at least 5 years and the contribution can be paid annually or monthly. A profit of 10% is added to the premiums payable. The insurance policies can be taken out by all persons living permanently inland.

17.5.1 Health insurance[118]

The only health insurance in the Social Market Economy is the General Health Insurance.[119] It is run by the Ministry of Health and includes accident and liability insurance. Those who derive 80% of their revenues from Social Market Economy companies do not have to pay a contribution. Accidents at work and occupational diseases are settled through the General Health Insurance. All Social Market Economy companies are

---

117 §217.3 Banks and insurance companies: BV Art. 98
118 §235,3 Health and accident insurance, §236,9,10 Health care: BV Art. 117a
119 Ministry of Health - 5.12.2 General Health Insurance

insured through the General Health Insurance. The General Health Insurance runs the health centres in the Social Villages and the state hospitals in the country. All persons earning 80% of their income in the Social Market Economy have unrestricted admission to health centres and state hospitals.
The General Health Insurance democratically votes with all contributors on which benefits from the fifth social security code[120] should be covered.

17.5.2 Parental insurance[121]

Anyone can join the parents' insurance. A membership of at least 5 years per child is obligatory. Both parents must take out a membership at least 2 months before the birth, the contribution years of which must have been completed by the age of 50. If the payment period has not been chosen by the parents themselves, it starts automatically on the basis of the data from the Persons Directory[122] on the age and number of children of the parent. If persons become parents after the age of 45, the payment period starts directly after the payment period. The parental insurance pays 80% of the insured parent's income per month for 2 years. The income is calculated from the revenues of the past 2 years. All revenues are added up, divided by 24 and 20% is deducted to calculate the monthly amount. The insurance company determines the revenues by making a digital request to the Ministry of Finance to find out the person's tax revenues. From this data of the past 2 tax years of the insured person, the income is calculated. For data protection reasons, the Ministry of Finance performs the above calculation and sends only the result to the insurance company.
The insurance company democratically votes with its members on the benefits. All insured persons can vote on the benefits every 2 years. The deciding factor is how many insured pay in for how long and how much is paid out for how long.
As a state-owned company of the Ministry of Social Market

120 http://www.gesetze-im-internet.de/sgb_5/
121 §234.5 Children's rights, child benefit and parental protection
122 Ministry of State Organisation - 4.6 Persons Directory

Economy, the insurance company earns 10% profits. Those who earn their income exclusively from Social Market Economy companies pay only 80% of the premiums due.

17.5.3 Unemployment insurance[123]

Unemployment insurance provides basic security for jobseekers through subsistence benefits. All companies in the Social Market Economy pay their compulsory unemployment insurance contributions through their business taxes. Unemployment insurance is a state enterprise of the Ministry of Social Market Economy. Social Market Economy contributions and declarations are regulated by the Unemployment Insurance Fund in voting with the Minister for Social Market Economy. The reports are made using data from the Labour Directory. All companies registered in the Social Market Economy that are owned by a person or in which a person is employed pay their taxes to the Ministry of Finance, which deducts contributions to the unemployment insurance fund from the business taxes.

Those who report themselves as unemployed in their Labour Directory profile and previously earned at least 80% of their income in Social Market Economy companies receive unemployment benefits. Insured persons receive a maximum of 12 months' unemployment benefit in the event of benefit, which corresponds to 80% of the average wage or profits of the past 2 years paid by the company or companies of the Social Market Economy.

You have 12 months to adjust your standard of living, save and pay off or cancel loans. Persons receiving unemployment insurance benefits are obliged to make use of the employment exchange services[124] free of charge. Payment of benefits ends as soon as a new job is taken up or 12 months have passed.

If after 10 months no employment contract has been signed or company has been founded, one has to apply for a place at the next Social Village. One can indicate in which Social

123§45,4 Welfare state, §232,1,2a,2b Occupational benefits: BV Art. 113
124Ministry of Labour - 12.2.1 Employment exchanges

Village one would prefer to live. Unemployment insurance makes compensation payments to the Ministry of Planned Economy[125] for unemployed people from the Social Market Economy who necessarily move to the Planned Economy.

The Social Market Economy unemployment insurance scheme democratically determines with all contributors which benefits from the Second and Third Social Code[126] should be taken over.

17.5.4 Pension insurance

The Ministry of Social Market Economy operates the pension insurance scheme and collects compulsory contributions from all persons who receive at least 80% of their income from companies in the Social Market Economy. The insured persons can determine the amount of compulsory contributions themselves by opting for different comfort classes, which provide for correspondingly different contribution rates.

The pension insurance operates retirement homes in different comfort classes. Contributors determine with the amount of their contributions in which comfort class they will live in their pension.

The low comfort class offers homes with Residential Communities and a health centre with medical care and outpatient care workers in rural holiday areas of the country.

The high comfort class offers cruise ships that are permanently on a world tour. The accommodation, supplies and care are quasi stationary and connect the services of a 5-star hotel and a university clinic. On these ships, the university clinic researches which diet, lifestyle and climate promote a long life and promote or alleviate age-related diseases. Immortality Health Insurance[127] is involved in the research costs.

---

125 Ministry of Planned Economy - 16.3.4 Compensation payments
126 http://www.gesetze-im-internet.de/sgb_2/ https://www.gesetze-im-internet.de/sgb_3/
127 Ministry of Health - 5.12.4 Immortality Health Insurance

17.5.5 Legal expenses insurance

Anyone who works in the Social Market Economy or owns a company there and receives at least 80% of his or her income from it pays into the legal protection insurance through the business tax. As long as one is employed or owns the company, one is insured. The legal expenses insurance covers any legal fees and court costs. The Ministry of Justice operates the state legal expenses insurance, which is compulsory insurance for members of the Planned Economy and Social Market Economy.[128]

17.5.6 Outage insurance

Money, goods and services are insured against failure in the Social Market Economy. If a service cannot be provided, another company in the Social Market Economy takes over the provision of the service at the agreed date and price. The outage insurance covers the additional costs or takes profits that lie between the agreed price and the price of the contracted company. If payments have already been made and the agreed service has not been provided, the outage insurance pays the costs to the accepting companies. The defaulting company is sued for damages by the Ministry of Social Market Economy to recover the costs. The owners of the defaulting companies are liable for this. If necessary, the company has to be sold, a loan taken out or the amount worked off in detention.

In the Social Market Economy, the customer always receives his agreed service and does not have to worry about legal disputes or finding a replacement. The companies of the Social Market Economy are in an alliance with each other in order to compensate for surplus demand or supply bottlenecks via other companies of the Social Market Economy.

How costs and profits are shared in such entrepreneurial social assistance is decided by the companies themselves. If no agreement can be reached, the Minister of the Ministry for Social Market Economy democratically settles the matter in a committee.

---

128 Ministry of Justice - 5.7.7 Legal expenses insurance

17.5.7 Downturn insurance[129]

The Ministry of Social Market Economy uses downturn insurance to coordinate economic policy and approve counter-cyclical tax burdens or relief.

The Ministry of Social Market Economy measures the strength and duration of a recovery through data from the Company Auditing Agency's economic auditors. The percentage increase in economic output increases the business tax accordingly. The increase in the percentage of business tax is transferred by the Ministry of Finance to the Ministry of Social Market Economy. The amount of money is saved and distributed back to the paying companies during downturns. Those who have paid in more will receive correspondingly more when they are distributed. The period and the amount of the monthly distributions are determined by the minister of the Social Market Economy or the affected citizens in a committee with a quorum of 40% or more. As far as possible, only the returns on the contributions saved are used in order to be able to maintain the payout for as long as possible.

18 Disaster management[130]

Social Market Economy companies are required to shift production in the event of a disaster in order to provide essential goods and services to the population. Essential goods and services include supporting the population with food, clothing, building materials, education, health, electricity and water. The Ministry of Security prepares an emergency plan[131] for each Social Market Economy company in cooperation with the Company Auditing Agency and affected citizens.

In situations of power-political threat, foreign trade can be restricted in whole or in part. The companies of the Social Market Economy can receive bans and bids to import or export. The sale of certain goods or services can also be banned or restricted inland at short notice.

In the event of war, the companies of the Social Market Economy are converted to a war economy. They produce

129 §150.4 Business taxes
130 §211 National supply: BV Art. 102
131 Ministry of Security - 5.7.3 Emergency plan

weapons, ammunition, war equipment and essential goods.

In severe shortages, all production is switched to essential goods. The enterprises receive their instructions like Planned Economy enterprises and businesses. If the situation allows, the entire population conducts a vote on demand and creates a digital duty roster with compulsory working hours in Social Market Economy companies.[132]

In the event of local natural disasters, volunteers and Social Market Economy waste management companies carry out clean-up work under the guidance of Ministry of Security staff. Reconstruction is carried out with the help of craft enterprises. Social Market Economy handicraft companies are gathered from all over the country in the event of a disaster. Their vehicles are loaded onto trains and transported to the disaster area with the workers. On the day of the disaster, emergency workers from the Ministry of Security and Social Market Economy waste management companies are sent to the disaster area. It usually takes one to two weeks for the clean-up work to be completed. During this time, handicraft enterprises can finish their orders or interrupt them for a period of time.[133] Other Social Market Economy handicraft enterprises take over the work according to the outage insurance. Collective orders for building materials are made for all disaster victims. The Ministry of Social Market Economy takes care of ordering, payment and delivery. The building material is provided by companies of the Social Market Economy or Planned Economy. If residents or companies want a different extension than the common standard of all affected citizens, they have to bear these costs themselves.

19 Switching to the new system

The template for the Social Market Economy is the social market economy of the Federal Republic of Germany, with the exception of social welfare. The Social Market Economy will adopt many German laws and parts of the social laws that have not been adopted in the Planned Economy. This applies

---

132 Ministry of Planned Economy - 7.3.1 Vote on demand, 7.6 Duty roster
133 Ministry of Security - 5.7.4 Reconstruction

especially to the rights of employees and self-employed sole traders.

Initially, the Social Market Economy and Free Market Economy are still united and are increasingly separated from each other by transferring the social laws to the Social Market Economy and the free trade laws to the Free Market Economy. The companies then choose one of the two economic forms. First, social welfare is removed from the Social Market Economy and transferred to the Planned Economy. Most compulsory insurance can continue in the Social Market Economy because it does not matter which economic form the contributors come from as long as they can pay their contributions. However, as soon as companies opt for the Social Market Economy, the insurance benefits become Tax-funded.

The insurance companies and the ministry hold committees to negotiate the changeover with the affected citizens, especially which contents from existing laws should be taken over or abolished.

19.1 Conversion of the old ministries

For the conversion of the old ministries, all departments and units of the old ministries that are changing to this ministry are identified. The organigrams are used to determine whether an entire department and all its units are changing or only individual units. All unsuitable departments and units are dropped. The existing staff adapts its tasks to the new requirements.

Contact form

Dear reader

If you would like to make what you have read come true, in whole or in part, together with other like-minded people, I offer you several possibilities with this contact form. Fill it out, tear out the page and send it by post to:

Andreas Seidl, P.O. Box 1206, 63488 Seligenstadt / Germany

Or send the details to:

Phone: 0049 1522 818 2243 (whatsapp, telegram, signal)

Email: andreas.seidl2022@web.de

Please mark with a cross:

O   I want to found a dynamic People's Party.

O   I want to donate money for implementation.

O   I want contacts with like-minded people in my area.

Forename: _____

Surname: _____

Please fill in only the contact option through which a reply should be made.

Street, house no.: _____

Postcode, city, country: _____

Phone: _____

Email address: _____